The Grey Mist:
a ghost story

Anthony Stamp

Beercott

The Grey Mist: a ghost story
A play in 2 acts

First Published in Great Britain in 2018 by Beercott Books.

ISBN: 978-1-9997429-4-2

A catalogue record of this book is available from the British Library.

Worldwide licence enquiries for this title should be directed to:

licensing@beercottbooks.co.uk.

Title subject to availability.

www.beercottbooks.co.uk

Beercott

CHARACTERS

DR TRENT: Respectable, modest practitioner in his late thirties or early forties

JULIA NORBURY: In her early thirties: neat, efficient, a little prim. She is assistant and administrator at the practice

KATE SIMPKINS: Indeterminate age, but probably in her forties: she is housemaid at the practice, a local with a country accent and a secretive air about her

CORBY: Oddjob man at the practice, of an indeterminate age: a local with a country accent and a blunt manner, shifty sometimes, secretive and dark. He is roughly dressed and unshaven

MRS MUMPKIN: A large and very talkative country woman

MR MUMPKIN: The small and bronchial husband, forever dominated by his wife

MRS PRYMM: An elderly twittering lady: she helps at the church and has an affectionate eye for Dr Trent

DR MORTIMER: Late fifties or early sixties, immaculately dressed senior doctor with an authoritative and supercilious manner

VERITY MANDRAKE: A ghost – in her twenties (when she died)

NARRATOR: In his fifties probably, smartly dressed: beyond this we need know nothing more about him

DENHAM: Doctor Mortimer's secretary: young, quiet and unassuming but efficient

MAUDE: A young lady who briefly passes through the surgery

SCENES

The play takes place in the consulting room of a small country practice in the 1920s

ACT 1

SCENE 1: Afternoon, around 4pm
SCENE 2: Morning, the following day
SCENE 3: Late morning, a week later
SCENE 4: Late evening, the same day
SCENE 5: Mid morning, several days later
SCENE 6: Late afternoon, the same day
SCENE 7: Around 10pm, the same day

ACT 2

SCENE 1: Afternoon, several days later
SCENE 2: Around 10pm, the same day
SCENE 3: Late afternoon, the following day
SCENE 4: Mid morning, the following day
SCENE 5: Evening, some days later
SCENE 6: Morning, the following day
SCENE 7: Mid afternoon, some time later

ACT 1:

Scene 1

The doctor's consulting room of a small country practice in the 1920s. There is a bookshelf on the DR wall containing a number of volumes of medical reference works and a large leather-bound photograph album. UR of the shelves is the doctor's desk with two chairs, one for the doctor and one for the patient. UR of the desk is a tall Grandfather clock, almost in the UR corner. In the corner of the wall, UR, is a narrow door or opening onto the set which should be hidden to the audience by the Grandfather clock.

In the rear wall is a double window with working curtains. The window should have handles though does not need to open. Part of a garden can be seen outside the window. There should be sufficient space between the window and backdrop to walk freely. R of the window an ordinary wooden chair stands against the wall. There may be a long wooden trunk below the window which can be used as a seat.

Against the wall UL stands a wooden filing cabinet. Down from this is a coat-stand. Down from this is a door, opening inwards and upstage, which leads to a hallway. A tiny portion of the hallway can be seen through the doorway. DL is a small round table with an armchair L and an ordinary wooden chair R. There are several lamps around the room which can be lit independently.

On the R stage extension there is an ornate desk. A comfortable-looking period office chair is behind it, its back to the wall. A second more standard chair is in front. There are a telephone, papers and a couple of books neatly stacked on the desk.

When the curtain rises the main stage is in semi-darkness. The extension is not lit. Actors on the main stage should already be in position. A single spotlight illuminates the Narrator who is seated on the arm of the easy chair front left. He wears a smoking jacket and addresses the audience.

NARRATOR: This story is about a haunting. It is a ghost story, if you like – whatever that may mean. I suspect it means different things to different people, to those who have experienced something and to those who have not. Some people may have naturally highly-tuned senses for these things while others remain in ignorance of them. I don't think it matters whether you believe in ghosts or not. That's just the way it is.

Now I'm a fairly practical sort of man. I would have put myself in the latter category. That's not to say I don't believe in ghosts. It's just that I had never had any experience of them. Well - not then anyway.

This – ghost story – came to me recently. Less than a year ago in fact. Parts of it were told to me. Other parts I discovered here and there, piece by piece. It concerns a doctor in a modest practice in a remote rural area of England in the 1920s. Like myself, I suspect that he was neither a believer or non-believer. He had simply never had cause to give the matter of ghosts and hauntings any thought. But certain circumstances, as you'll see, changed all that. And although these events took place quite recently, the story really begins many years earlier.

The NARRATOR breaks off. He is still and silent for a moment. Suddenly he emits a fearful gasp and stands. He shivers.

NARRATOR: It's coming now. Yes, it's coming. I can feel it. It's like ice-cold fingers brushing against my spine. Like an icy draft breathing on my neck. It's coming. Yes. It's beginning now...

Spotlight blacks out and the NARRATOR exits as the lights come up on the main stage. JULIA NORBURY is alone in the consulting room, making final adjustments to various items: straightening items on the desk, re-angling a picture slightly on the wall, touching at the curtains to correctly align them.

JULIA is in her early thirties, neat, efficient and a little prim. She is assistant and administrator at the practice.

She runs a finger along the window-sill, notices dust and is not pleased.

KATE SIMPKINS enters from the LH door. KATE is the housemaid. Her age is indeterminate, probably forties. She is local and speaks with a country accent. She has a generally secretive air at all times.

JULIA: Simpkins, the window sill has not been dusted properly.

KATE: No, miss?

JULIA: No. It's thick with dust.

KATE: Yes, miss?

JULIA: Well see to it now.

KATE: Yes, miss.

KATE pulls a duster from her pocket and goes to the window. She glances slyly at Julia to be sure she is unobserved, then gives the sill a few insolent flicks. JULIA is examining the room.

JULIA: What time is it, Simpkins?

KATE: Just before four, miss.

JULIA: Have you got the tea things ready?

KATE: Yes, miss.

JULIA: Dr Trent will be glad of refreshment when he arrives. It's such a tedious train journey up from London and then quite a walk from the station.

KATE: Could have sent Corby to the station to fetch him in the dog-cart.

JULIA gives KATE a look of contempt at the idea.

JULIA: Yes, well hardly. In any case Dr Mortimer said in his letter that Dr Trent would be quite happy to walk.

KATE: Well that settles the matter then, don't it, miss?

JULIA (*glancing around again anxiously*): I do hope everything is in order.

KATE: What's he like, miss? This Dr Trent.

JULIA: I know little more than what Dr Mortimer put in his letter. He's young, unmarried, currently a junior doctor attached to Dr Mortimer's practice. (*Pause*) I know I haven't been here very long myself –

KATE: Four months, b'ain't it, miss?

JULIA: Yes, about that. But something puzzles me.

KATE: What's that then, miss?

JULIA: Well the former doctor, Dr Evans –

KATE: God rest his soul.

JULIA: Yes. Quite. Well he was supplied by Dr Mortimer's London practice too, wasn't he?

KATE (*suddenly evasive*): I don't think he worked for the practice...

JULIA: No, possibly not, but his post here was arranged through Dr Mortimer, I understand.

KATE: Maybe...

JULIA: I'm certain it was. He mentioned it once, I'm sure.

KATE: Couldn't say, miss.

JULIA: Not that I had much chance to get to know him, poor man. He seemed nice enough but something played on his mind.

KATE: Can't say I noticed, miss.

JULIA: He began to look quite haggard – almost haunted – by the end...

KATE looks at her sharply but says nothing.

JULIA: I often wonder what could have been worrying him so much. Surely not the running of this practice. It's hardly onerous work afterall. A nice country practice. Gentle flow of patients. Still, I suppose one never really knows another person that well.

KATE: No, miss.

JULIA comes from her reverie and pulls herself together.

JULIA: Well. This isn't getting things done. What time is it now?

KATE: Just on four, miss.

JULIA: Then we can expect Dr Trent at any moment.

The sound of a door-knocker is heard.

KATE: Spect that'll be new doctor now, miss.

JULIA: Prospective new doctor, Simpkins.

KATE: Yes, miss. I'll let him in.

KATE exits via the LH door. JULIA quickly checks around the room once more. She glances into a mirror and minutely adjusts her hair.

A moment later DR TRENT is shown into the room by KATE. He is pleasant-looking, aged in his thirties or early forties.

KATE: Dr Trent.

TRENT steps forward and shakes hands with JULIA. KATE watches from just inside the door.

TRENT: Miss Norbury?

JULIA: Dr Trent. How do you do?

TRENT: How do you do?

JULIA: I hope you had no trouble finding us.

TRENT: No, none at all. It's a straight walk from the railway station.

JULIA: And how was your train journey?

TRENT: Well, you know what these branch line railways are like.

JULIA: Yes. Quite. I expect you would like some tea.

TRENT: Yes, tea would be very nice, thankyou.

JULIA: Simpkins?

KATE: Yes, miss.

KATE gives them one final quick searching glance then leaves the room. JULIA and TRENT stand in brief awkward silence alone in the room.

JULIA: Please, let me take your coat.

TRENT: Thankyou.

He removes his overcoat which Julia takes to hang on the coatstand next to the LH door. As she returns she begins to point out features of the room.

JULIA: This is the consulting room. The medicine chest. The examination couch. Shelves of reference books. Your – that is, the doctor's chair and desk.

TRENT: It all looks very organised.

Trent goes to the bookshelves and briefly scans some of the titles.

TRENT: Plenty of reading matter here.

JULIA: I'm afraid each doctor tends to bring his own collection with him and then they just get left –

JULIA stops herself, as if she has realised she was about to say something unadvisable.

JULIA: The shelves could do with a good clear-out, I expect.

TRENT: Yes, I'm sure.

Another brief silence between them.

TRENT: You received Dr Mortimer's letter?

JULIA: Yes. He told us to expect you.

TRENT: I have to let him know my decision tomorrow. Though in actual fact I don't really think –

He is interrupted by KATE's return with a tray of tea things. While she and JULIA arrange them on the small table front left, TRENT drifts to the window to look out. He notices the window sill, wipes his finger along it and then inspects the dust on his finger. He glances quickly back at the two ladies then hurriedly wipes the dust from his finger on his jacket.

By now the tea things are placed and JULIA dismisses KATE.

JULIA: Thankyou, Simpkins.

KATE executes a half-hearted curtsey and leaves the room. She has a good look at TRENT as she goes.

JULIA: Please come and sit down, Dr Trent.

TRENT: Thankyou.

They seat themselves either side of the small table. JULIA pours tea while they talk.

TRENT: Are there many staff here?

JULIA: Other than myself there is just Kate Simpkins who you just met...

TRENT: Housemaid, I imagine?

JULIA: That's right, and general domestic duties. She's a local, been here for years. Efficient enough. (*TRENT glances discreetly at the windowsill then quickly back to JULIA.*)

JULIA: The only other is Mr Corby. He's – well – a handyman, I suppose you'd call him. Oddjob man. Tends the garden, does repairs – that sort of thing. Another local who's been here as long as Simpkins, if not longer... He's a – well a strange sort – but useful to have around and he does his job well so...

TRENT notices the slight hesitation in JULIA's manner during this.

TRENT: I suppose it takes the locals some time to get used to outsiders. Something I shall have to prepare myself for, if I decide to take up the position.

JULIA: They can be a close-knit lot to begin with.

TRENT: How long have you been here, Miss Norbury?

JULIA: About four months only. I'm still an outsider too, you see.

TRENT: Yes. Well I shall look forward to meeting Mr Corby from what you say.

JULIA: Yes. (*Pause*) You were beginning to say just now about deciding if you would accept the offer...?

TRENT: Oh yes. I was a little surprised when Dr Mortimer made the suggestion I come out here. I am only a meagre cog in the works of his practice. I haven't been there long. I would have expected him to offer this chance to one of his more experienced doctors. Unless, of course, he just wants to get rid of me.

They laugh.

JULIA: I'm sure it isn't that.

TRENT: Probably not. But all the same I was a little puzzled at his choosing me.

JULIA: Perhaps you can ask him about it tomorrow.

TRENT: Yes, perhaps I will. Although he is not really the sort of man you question lightly. I got the distinct feeling that if I refused he'd put me on the back shelf for good.

JULIA: Oh I'm sure he wouldn't do that.

TRENT: You don't know him. What is the practice like – the patients, I mean?

JULIA: They're mostly typical country folk, nice enough on the whole.

TRENT: And one or two...?

JULIA: Well one or two who may take a bit of getting used to, yes. Most of them visit during surgery hours, though you'll be expected to make some house-calls as well.

TRENT: I'm sure I can cope with that. I imagine most of them are from the village I saw near the railway station.

JULIA: If you can call it a village. It's little more than a few houses really, and a shop and a public house. There are a few farms too.

TRENT: It all sounds quite manageable.

JULIA: Yes...

There is a moment's silence. They finish their tea.

JULIA: Perhaps you would like to see the rest of the house now?

TRENT: Yes, thankyou.

They stand.

JULIA: There are the out-buildings and the garden. And then, I expect, you'll be wanting to start back.

TRENT: There are still plenty trains to London.

JULIA: (*indicating the window*) Yes, but it's starting to get dark already. And you have that walk to the station.

TRENT: I don't mind walking in the dark.

JULIA: The road to the station is little more than a narrow lane in places and quite unlit. It can be quite – treacherous – in darkness. The tour will not take long and then you can be on your way.

TRENT: Very well. Lead the way.

> *JULIA goes to the LH door. TRENT follows, taking his overcoat from the stand. He pauses in the doorway after Julia has exited and glances back around the room. His brief smile suggests that he is taking to the idea of working here. He exits.*

> *There are a few moments of stillness. The lighting will dim very slowly throughout this next sequence as if dusk is drawing in outside. KATE enters the room from the LH door and sees that it is empty. She goes towards the table bearing the tea things and begins to collect them up onto a tray. Then she hesitates. She looks towards the bookshelves beyond the desk then goes uncertainly over to them. Her manner is both furtive and nervous. She pauses in front of the shelves, glances back to the door to be certain she is alone, then very gingerly pulls a large leather-bound photograph album from its place on the second shelf. She holds it nervously, staring at it as if afraid of it, then summoning her courage lays it carefully on the desk. She hesitates again. Then she opens the cover, and slowly turns some pages as if frightened of what she may see.*

> *The voices of TRENT and JULIA are heard suddenly off.*

TRENT (*off*): Thankyou for showing me around, Miss Norbury. And for the tea. I'm sure I shall see you again soon.

JULIA (*off*): Goodbye, Dr Trent. Please take care on your way back to the station.

> *The sound of the front door closing is heard.*

> *KATE closes the photograph album hurriedly and quickly returns it to the shelf. She looks around in panic as JULIA's footsteps are heard returning, and hurries to stand behind the*

LH door. JULIA enters through this door a moment later. The room has grown dim. JULIA does not notice KATE. JULIA moves to the centre of the room and stands smiling with gentle satisfaction, thinking of DR TRENT. Then realises how dark the room has become and comes from her reverie. She goes to the desk and turns on a lamp. She notices the tea things still uncollected on the table, tuts to herself and goes over to the table.

KATE: I were just clearing those away, miss.

Julia lets out a short scream of fear and surprise.

JULIA: Simpkins! What are you doing here?

KATE: Just drawing the curtains, miss.

JULIA: Well I wish you wouldn't creep around like that!

KATE draws the curtains while JULIA tries to control her breathing. KATE comes to the table and finishes collecting the tea things onto the tray.

KATE: That Dr Trent – he's quite a looker, b'ain't he? Is he going to take the job?

JULIA (*frostily*): He hasn't made up his mind yet. We shall just have to wait and see.

KATE: Yes, miss.

JULIA: Now get those tea things cleared away and then find Corby if you would and tell him we shall need more logs for the fire.

KATE: Yes, miss.

KATE bobs a slightly sarcastic curtsey, then leaves the room with the tray.

JULIA watches her go. Then her haughty expression becomes wistful as she moves to the centre of the room and tilts her head to one side.

JULIA (*softly to herself*): Quite a looker.

Scene 2

Lights fade on main stage and come up on Dr Mortimer's Office set on the LH extension.

The office comprises an impressive oak desk, a chair to either side. Some papers, books and a telephone are on the desk. A large portrait of an austere and somewhat rakish Victorian gentleman hangs on the wall. DR MORTIMER is seated behind his desk, writing a report, when TRENT enters. Mortimer is in his late fifties, immaculately dressed and supercilious and authoritative in manner.

There is a brief knock at a door and DENHAM enters. He is Mortimer's secretary, smartly dressed, quiet in disposition but efficient.

DENHAM: Dr Trent is here, Dr Mortimer.

MORTIMER: Very well, Denham. Show him in.

DENHAM: Very well, sir.

> *DENHAM exits. MORTIMER seems ill at ease. He glances at the portrait on the wall. He straightens an item or two on his desk nervously, then with a visible effort composes himself.*

> *DENHAM enters with TRENT.*

DENHAM: Dr Trent, sir.

MORTIMER: Thank you, Denham.

DENHAM: Will that be all, sir?

MORTIMER: Tea, if you'd be so kind..

DENHAM: Very good, sir. For two?

MORTIMER: For one.

> *DENHAM throws a brief doubtful glance between MORTIMER and TRENT then exits.*

MORTIMER stares at the desk. He does not look up for several moments. TRENT stands awkwardly. Finally he raises his head.

MORTIMER: Dr Trent. Thankyou for coming. Take a seat.

TRENT sits in the chair opposite MORTIMER. He has his medical bag and his overcoat draped awkwardly over his knees and looks uncomfortable.

MORTIMER: You have been to visit the country medical practice, I understand? What is your opinion? Is it to your liking?

TRENT: It seems very agreeable, yes.

MORTIMER: Then you will accept the position?

TRENT: Well, yes. I would be more than happy –

MORTIMER: Dr Evans built up a good practice there. He was well regarded by his patients and the locality alike. His untimely death – his...untimely death –

MORTIMER falters, seems momentarily unable to finish the sentence. Fear shows in his expression for a fleeting moment.

TRENT: Dr Mortimer?

MORTIMER regains his composure with effort and continues:

MORTIMER: His untimely death will be a sad loss to the community. You will have a lot to live up to, Dr Trent. I hope I can rely on you.

TRENT: Yes, I understand. I shall do my best. But -

MORTIMER: But?

TRENT: I must confess, Dr Mortimer, to being somewhat surprised at being your first choice for this position. Of course I am flattered and honoured. But I am still just a junior partner in this practice and would have expected –

MORTIMER: Do you wish to decline the position?

TRENT: No, sir, no. Not at all. I simply thought that someone with greater experience – perhaps you yourself, sir?

MORTIMER (*stiffening*): That would not be possible at all. My place is here.

TRENT: Yes, I see that but –

MORTIMER (*firmly*): Not possible at all.

There is a moment's awkward silence. Then MORTIMER relaxes a little.

MORTIMER: You are not married, Dr Trent. You have no dependents, I believe?

TRENT: That is correct, sir.

MORTIMER: Then that makes you – ideal for the position. Nothing to delay your departure, d'you see?

TRENT: I understand.

MORTIMER: Then that is settled. You shall commence duties at the new practice just as soon as it is convenient for you to do so.

MORTIMER stands, indicating that the interview is over. TRENT gets to his feet. MORTIMER shakes his hand across the desk.

MORTIMER: Congratulations and good luck, Dr Trent.

TRENT: Thankyou.

TRENT exits.

The moment he has gone MORTIMER'S expression crumbles – becomes perplexed and fearful. He sinks back in his chair then takes a small bottle of pills from his pocket and puts one in his mouth.

DENHAM enters with a tray of tea things. MORTIMER hides the bottle of pills and hastily assumes a businesslike manner.

DENHAM: Your tea, sir.

MORTIMER: Thank you, Denham.

DENHAM arranges the tea things on the desk.

DENHAM: Has Dr Trent gone?

MORTIMER (*defeated*): Yes. Yes, Dr Trent has gone.

DENHAM (*anxiously*): Dr Mortimer? Are you alright?

MORTIMER (*authoritive again*): Yes yes. Of course. Thank you, Denham. That will be all.

DENHAM exits.

MORTIMER sees that he has gone and his shoulders slump. He stares sightlessly into the distance, then he looks again at the portrait on the wall for several moments. Facing forwards, he puts his head in his hands.

Black out on side stage.

Scene 3

Spotlight only illuminates THE NARRATOR who perches on the arm of the chair Left of main stage.

NARRATOR: And so within the week Dr Trent had established himself in his new environment and, immediately fully occupied by the many new faces and routines he had to learn, the misgivings he experienced when offered the post now hardly entered his head. He was happy with the decision he had made and invigorated by the challenges he faced each day. The curious interview he had had with Dr Mortimer was entirely forgotten. For now.

> *Spotlight fades on THE NARRATOR, who exits the stage. Lights come up on the main stage.*
>
> *TRENT is at his desk with a patient, MRS PRYMM, a lady of later years who watches his every move with obvious fascination. He is bringing the consultation to an end. The photograph album from the bookshelf is now on the floor out of sight beyond the desk.*

TRENT: Well, Mrs Prymm, I'm afraid I have to tell you that my verdict is this.... There is absolutely nothing wrong with you. Your health is fine.

> *MRS PRYMM titters with exaggerated coyness.*

MRS PRYMM: Oh Doctor! You are a tease! Leading me on like that!

TRENT: It's perfectly true, Mrs Prymm. You're fit as a fiddle. Strong as an ox.

MRS PRYMM: Are you absolutely certain, Doctor? You can't find anything at all wrong with me?

TRENT: You are in very good health.

MRS PRYMM: Well...

There is a silence during which MRS PRYMM continues to gaze
wistfully at TRENT. TRENT begins to feel slightly
uncomfortable. He shuffles papers in a concluding manner. He
folds up the tubes of his stethoscope with exaggerated finality.
Eventually MRS PRYMM takes the hint.

MRS PRYMM: Well then...

TRENT: Thankyou, Mrs Prymm.

MRS PRYMM (*rising*): Thank-you, Doctor.

MRS PRYMM starts for the LH door. In the middle of the room
she stops, wincing in an exaggerated fashion, holding her leg.
She turns back.

MRS PRYMM: Ooooh!

TRENT: Mrs Prymm?

MRS PRYMM: It my leg, doctor. Plays me up terribly in this
    weather. It's all the walking I do, you see. For the church.
    Are you a church-goer yourself, doctor?

TRENT: Well – .

MRS PRYMM: A wonderful church-going community we have
    here, doctor. And a wonderful vicar. Have you met him? But
    of course the church itself – wonderful church – is badly in
    need of restoration, as they always are. The vicar and I are
    always on the look-out for new ways to raise funds to
    support its upkeep. But it does entail a lot of walking
    naturally. And we are always keen to enlist new blood, as it
    were, to help us – .

She pauses, gazing significantly and wistfully at TRENT. The
significance is not lost on him. He clears his throat.

TRENT: Yes, yes. I'm sure it must be – .

MRS PRYMM: Perhaps you would like to lend a hand too, doctor. Just what we need, you know. A fit young man like yourself to help out.

TRENT: Well -

MRS PRYMM: There's always so much to be done what with the annual jumble sale and the bonny baby competition and the collecting and carrying and so on.

TRENT: Well I'll see. Perhaps when I'm more settled in – .

MRS PRYMM: Oh that's wonderful, doctor! Simply wonderful! I knew we could rely on you!

TRENT: Yes, yes. And now – .

MRS PRYMM: Oh of course, of course. I'm sure you have plenty to do yourself and I'm taking up your time!

TRENT: Good morning, Mrs Prymm.

MRS PRYMM: Good morning, doctor. I so look forward to having you with us in our endless fight against the dry-rot and crumbling foundations!

MRS PRYMM heads for the door. Her step is now sprightly – there is no sign of her former leg problem. She glances back coyly several times and seems on the point of returning when she meets JULIA who enters carrying a cup of tea.

JULIA: Good morning, Mrs Prymm.

MRS PRYMM: Oh! Good morning, Miss Norbury.

JULIA: Do take care on your way home. The air is chilly today.

MRS PRYMM (*shooting one final glance at TRENT*): If I were to get a cold on my chest I'm sure Doctor Trent would look after me.

JULIA: Quite.

MRS PRYMM: Well then. Good day.

MRS PRYMM finally leaves. JULIA closes the door behind her and carries the cup and saucer to TRENT. TRENT visibly relaxes.

JULIA: That was your last patient for this morning, doctor.

TRENT: Thank goodness! I thought she was never going to leave!

JULIA: I've brought you some tea.

TRENT: Thankyou. Most welcome!

He takes it from her and drinks gratefully.

TRENT: I hope there aren't too many more like Mrs Prymm. How long have I been here? A week? And she's made three appointments already! And there's nothing wrong with her. I've never seen such a case of hypochondria!

JULIA: I think it might be a little more than that.

TRENT: How do you mean?

JULIA: I suspect there may be a touch of hero-worship too.

TRENT: What!

TRENT stares at JULIA in dawning horror, then they both laugh. For a moment then it is as if there is a bond between them: they find each other attractive. But neither likes to express the emotion. TRENT drinks his tea again.

TRENT: Well, as I said – I hope there aren't too many more patients like her.

JULIA: Some of them are a bit odd and take some getting use to.

TRENT: It's a very different climate to the one I came from.

JULIA: The patients seem to have taken to you.

TRENT: Mrs Prymm certainly has.

JULIA: She's an extreme case, I know. But the others – they seem to – like you –

TRENT: Really?

JULIA: Yes.

Again there's a brief awkward moment that each of them senses. TRENT finishes his tea and hands back the cup and saucer.

TRENT: Just what the doctor ordered! Thankyou.

JULIA: Well – I must get on.

JULIA turns to go.

TRENT (*hesitantly*): Miss Norbury?

JULIA: Yes?

TRENT: I'd quite like a spot of fresh air after a morning with the sick and needy. I thought to take a walk after lunch. Perhaps you'd – care to accompany me?

JULIA (*pleased but suppressing it*): Oh – yes. Thankyou. We have some pleasant countryside around and a very pretty church.

TRENT: Good. After lunch then.

JULIA moves towards the door. TRENT gets up and goes to the window. He notices something outside.

TRENT: Hello! Who's that?

JULIA pauses by the door.

JULIA: What is it?

TRENT: There's a young lady standing on the pathway outside.

JULIA: Young lady?

There is a very slight tensing in her bearing. The tea-cup rattles briefly against the saucer. She stays at the door.

TRENT: She's just standing there staring towards the house. Not moving. I wonder if she's a patient frightened to come in.

JULIA: What – what does she look like?

TRENT: It's hard to see. The sun's behind her. Quite tall. Young, I should say – twenties probably. Long grey dress to the ground. I – I can't see her face because of the sun. Perhaps I should go out to her.

JULIA: D'you think that's a good idea?

TRENT: Well if she's nervous of coming in...

JULIA: It might scare her all the more.

TRENT: It's strange. She's so still. I don't think I've ever seen anybody quite so immobile. Perhaps I should open the window and call to her.

TRENT reaches for the window catch. JULIA drops the cup and saucer which smash loudly in the quiet room.

JULIA (*urgently*): Don't!

TRENT looks around, then goes to JULIA.

TRENT: What is it?

JULIA: Stupid of me. It slipped through my fingers. What a mess on the floor.

TRENT: Soon clear that up.

JULIA (*stooping to collect the broken china*): I'm not usually so clumsy. You must think me an idiot!

TRENT: Of course not. I have days like that too. (*Pause*) I wonder
who she is and what she wants.

*TRENT drifts back to the window and looks out again. JULIA
stands, holding the fragments of china.*

TRENT: I can't see her now. She's gone from the path.

JULIA: Changed her mind perhaps.

TRENT: Or come to the door. I'll go and look.

*TRENT hurries out of the LH door before JULIA can speak. She
stands alone for moment. She looks deeply concerned. She
glances towards the window, and drawing a deep breath, goes
tentatively over to it. She hesitates, as if frightened to look out.
As she approaches it TRENT re-enters the room.*

TRENT: There's no sign of her.

JULIA: Oh?

TRENT: I went along the path to the gate and around the side of
the house, but she'd gone.

JULIA: Well I'm sure she'll come back when she's made up her
mind.

TRENT: Wonder who she is.

JULIA: I'd better get rid of this smashed china.

*JULIA exits via the LH door. TRENT looks again through the
window then sits at his desk. He is lost in thought for moment,
still puzzled by the girl he has seen. Then he notices something
on the floor beyond the desk. It is the leather-bound photograph
album that Kate was seen holding earlier. It appears to have
fallen from its place on the shelf. TRENT picks it up and
considers it briefly. He notices the gap on the shelf.*

TRENT: Now how did you get down there?

He is on the point of returning it to its rightful place when he stops. He shivers slightly. He stares again at the album as if it suddenly has some meaning for him that he cannot understand. Tentatively he goes to open the cover.

KATE enters through the LH door. She has a mop and bucket.

KATE: Miss Norbury sent me along. Said summat got spilled –

She seems to freeze as she notices the album in TRENT'S hands.

TRENT: Oh it's nothing much. Some dregs of tea, that's all.

He holds the album for a moment longer – while KATE watches him – then seems to forget what he was about to do and slides it back into its place on the shelf. KATE immediately gets to work with the mop. TRENT resumes his seat at the desk.

TRENT: You didn't by any chance see a young lady outside just now, did you?

KATE: Young lady, sir?

TRENT: I saw her from the window, just standing on the pathway staring at the house. I thought she must be a patient frightened to come in.

KATE: No, sir. I b'ain't seen nobody, sir. I been round the back, see, most of the morning.

TRENT: Ah well. I dare say she'll try again.

KATE (*uneasily*): Dare say she will, sir.

KATE has finished mopping and collects together mop and bucket.

KATE: Lunch be in ten minutes.

TRENT: Thankyou, Kate.

KATE exits the room.

TRENT remains seated for a moment longer then returns to look out of the window.

CORBY enters from the LH door. He is of indeterminate age, roughly dressed in shirt, trousers and opened waistcoat. He wears a battered top hat incongruously on his head. He has a stubble from several days without bothering to shave. His manner is like that of KATE but more so – secretive, shifty, dark.

TRENT turns, sensing him.

CORBY: Doctor?

TRENT: Ah Mr Corby.

CORBY: No Mister. Just Corby.

TRENT: Yes, well – .

CORBY: Heard you were asking after me.

TRENT: Yes, yes, that's right. Take a seat.

CORBY: I'm alright.

TRENT: As you wish. I've had little chance to speak to you since I've been here. I thought we should have a chat.

CORBY: 'Bout what like?

TRENT: Well – nothing in particular. About what you do, for example.

CORBY: Summat wrong with what I do, is there?

TRENT: No, no. Not at all. I just wondered about the extent of your duties. I wouldn't want to ask you to do anything that is outside your remit.

TRENT'S attempt at light humour is lost on CORBY who stares back at him suspiciously. Realising this, TRENT tries again:

TRENT: Could you explain to me what your duties are?

CORBY: Bit of everything, like.

TRENT: Yes? For example?

CORBY: Fetching, carrying, mending, garden. Cleaning up the mess your patients leave behind. Clear away the bodies too, sometimes.

TRENT (*slightly alarmed*): Yes, well – I trust I shan't cause you to do that too often!

CORBY: You'd be surprised. 'Specially during the season.

TRENT: The season?

CORBY: Grey Mist season they calls it round here.

TRENT: I'm sorry? Grey Mist season? What's that? A local name for some kind of seasonal infection?

CORBY: Aye. That's one way of describing it.

TRENT: What does it consist of? I mean – what are the symptoms?

KATE (*off*): Lunch!

> *CORBY looks as if he realises he has said too much and clams up.*

CORBY: Lunchtime. (*He turns to leave.*)

TRENT: Oh Mr Cor – Corby. There's something else I wanted to ask you.

> *CORBY halts again a few paces away. He does not turn back to face TRENT.*

TRENT: A little earlier I saw a young lady standing outside on the path looking at the house. Did you happen to notice her?

CORBY (*now very guarded*): Young lady?

TRENT: Tall, slim. Wearing a long grey dress, I think.

> *CORBY does not reply. He carefully keeps his back turned to TRENT but we can see his face tightening subtly.*

TRENT: I am worried that she was a patient afraid to come in for some reason. I wondered if you'd seen her – if you might know who she is.

CORBY: I were round back, sir. Choppin' wood for your fire. I b'ain't seen no-one, young lady or any other.

TRENT: Oh, I see. Very well.

KATE (*off, more impatient*): Lunch!

CORBY: Best get off.

TRENT: Well if you do happen to see someone like that near the cottage, please come and tell me.

CORBY gives a curt nod then leaves the room.

TRENT seems a bit nonplussed by CORBY'S attitude, but after a moment shrugs it off. He goes once more to the window and looks out.

KATE (*off, bellowed*): Lunch!!

TRENT (*to himself*): Yes, yes, alright. I'm coming.

TRENT leaves the window and exits the room.

Black out.

Scene 4

Lights come up partially.

It is late in the evening. Low wind can be heard moaning outside.The lights of the consulting room are turned low, creating a shadowy atmosphere. TRENT is dozing in the armchair front left. There are the dregs of a glass of port and a plate with the remains of some cheese and biscuits on the small table next to him.

After a few moments of this a woman's voice is heard whimpering softly. (The voice is VERITY'S.) The sound is strangely disembodied so that it is hard to tell where it comes from.

TRENT stirs restlessly in the chair but does not wake.

The woman's whimpering is heard again, a little louder.

TRENT wakes suddenly with a start. He sits forward. He shivers. He looks warily around the room but it is empty. He gets up from the chair and instinctively goes over to the window, pulls back the curtain and peers out into the blackness. He can see nothing and nobody out there. He turns back into the room, clearly disturbed – looks around it again as if expecting to see somebody. He shivers again then shakes his head in confusion.

He looks at the grandfather clock beyond the desk and checks his own watch, realising it is late. He goes to the desk to switch off the lamp there, but notices the photograph album which is once more on the floor in front of the shelves. Curiously he picks it up, lays it on the desk and opens it. It contains a number of portraits and group photos – many of people in Victorian dress. He turns the pages slowly, glancing at the photos. He stops on a particular page, his attention caught by one photo of a young woman.

From somewhere comes a woman's voice, distant and plaintive:

VERITY (*off*): Help me.

> *TRENT straightens in shock, the album forgotten. He stares around the room. He listens but there is silence.*
>
> *KATE enters the room from the LH door.*

KATE: You still up, doctor? 'Tis nearly midnight.

TRENT: What? Yes.

KATE: You alright, sir?

TRENT: What? Yes, yes. I fell asleep. Came around with a bit of a start.

KATE: You finished with this? (*indicating the glass and plate on the table*)

TRENT: Yes. Thankyou.

KATE goes to collect the things from the table. TRENT is still clearly disturbed by the voice.

TRENT: Kate – you didn't – you didn't call out just now, did you?

KATE: Call out, sir?

TRENT: A few moments ago.

KATE: No, sir. Not me, sir.

TRENT: Did you hear someone? A – a woman's voice?

KATE: B'ain't heard nothing, sir, 'cept the odd owl. And this wind. Whistles round this old building something terrible it do, sometimes. All sorts of noises it do make then. You gets used to it in time and don't hear it no more. But you being new like...

TRENT: Ah. Yes. You're probably right. Maybe that's what it was then. Just the wind. Or an owl.

KATE has the glass and plate in her hands. She glances at them significantly.

KATE: You ask me, sir, you should lay off the cheese just afore bedtime.

TRENT (*forcing a smile*): Yes. That's probably good advice, Kate.

He starts to tidy the room and switch off lights.

KATE: I'll do that for you, doctor. You get yourself off to bed.

TRENT: Thankyou. Goodnight.

KATE: Goodnight, doctor.

TRENT leaves the room. KATE listens to hear his tread on the stairs then goes quickly to the desk where the photo album still lays open. She puts down the glass and plate and returns to the LH door and calls in an urgent whisper:

KATE: Corby! Corby!

CORBY (*off*): What is it, woman?

KATE: Quiet! Get in here, you great lummox!

She goes back to the desk and stares at the open album. After a moment CORBY enters by the LH door. He looks put out at having been summoned.

CORBY: What d'you want, woman?

KATE: Quiet! Keep your voice down! Come here!

CORBY goes to where she stands near the desk.

CORBY: What is it?

KATE: Look.

They stare at the open album.

CORBY: Well?

KATE: See the page it's opened at? See the picture?

CORBY (*resigned, practical*): I see it.

KATE: You know what it means, don't you? You know what this means?

CORBY: Course I do, woman. But there b'aint't no use our worrying about it. You knows that.

CORBY closes the album and pushes it back into its place on the shelf.

KATE: He said he heard a voice too. Woman's voice. It's happening again, b'ain't it? It's happening again.

CORBY: Yes. Happening again.

KATE: When will it end?

CORBY: You knows the answer to that one as well as I do, woman. Now come on. It's late. I'm going to bed.

CORBY gives her a final look then leaves the room. KATE, left alone, looks again at the album on the shelf then moves to the centre of the room.

KATE (*fearfully to herself*): It's happening again.

Black out.

Scene 5

Spotlight illuminates the NARRATOR who is seated in the armchair front left.

NARRATOR: Several days went by without incident. Dr Trent, now into his second or third week at his new practice, began to relax and feel more settled. His life was taking on a reassuring routine.

Spotlight goes out and NARRATOR exits. Lights come up on stage. It is a brightly lit morning. MRS PRYMM is seated once again with TRENT at his desk. TRENT displays good-humoured patience as he manoeuvres the consultation to a close.

MRS PRYMM: Oh my legs are so bad again today, doctor. All that walking I've had to do. Organising things for the church restoration fund. On my own.

TRENT: Yes, I'm sure, Mrs Prymm. I expect it's partly the weather though. Just take the tablets I prescribed for you, and the surgical stockings should help.

MRS PRYMM: You'll want to see me again, I expect? To check on my progress?

TRENT: Come back in two weeks, Mrs Prymm.

MRS PRYMM: As long as that?

TRENT: That should be ample time for the tablets to take effect.

MRS PRYMM: But what if I have a relapse?

TRENT: If that should happen then by all means come back and see me sooner.

MRS PRYMM: Oh thankyou, doctor.

TRENT: My pleasure.

MRS PRYMM: You haven't forgotten our little arrangement, I hope?

TRENT: Arangement?

MRS PRYMM: Your assistance with our fund-raising activities?

TRENT: Oh. No, no, of course not. But I have been rather busy so –

MRS PRYMM: Vicar was so delighted when I told him we had a new recruit.

TRENT: He was?

MRS PRYMM: Oh delighted! So I hope we shall see you very soon. We have a collection bucket all ready for you!

TRENT: That's very kind of you. In the meantime take the tablets as I've prescribed them. Good morning, Mrs Prymm.

MRS PRYMM: Good morning, doctor.

TRENT and MRS PRYMM stand. TRENT escorts her to the door while she twitters endless gratitudes up into his face. He eases her out of the door, draws a long breath then calls through the door:

TRENT: Next, please.

TRENT resumes his seat at the desk. After a brief moment MR AND MRS MUMPKIN enter. They are a typical country couple. MR MUMPKIN is small and bronchial. He wears a cloth cap and a muffler is wound around his neck. He says very little but often wheezes. MRS MUMPKIN is large and very talkative – the dominant partner. She wears a 'Sunday Best' hat as a sign of respect because she is visiting a doctor.

There is a considerable amount of bustle in their entrance: MRS MUMPKIN feels the need to guide her husband into the room, though he is no doubt more than capable on his own.

TRENT stands quickly as they bundle towards him. MR MUMPKIN is deposited in the patient's chair. MRS MUMPKIN looks pointedly around for a chair for herself. TRENT finds an upright chair from a corner which he places a little way off. MRS MUMPKIN moves it as close to the desk as she can then sits squarely between them.

TRENT: Good morning. How can I help you – ?

MRS MUMPKIN: It's my Arthur, doctor – Arthur Mumpkin.

TRENT: Mr Mumpkin.

MRS MUMPKIN: Terrible wheezing and groaning he got on his chest, he do. Terrible bad of a night-time. Hardly sleeps a wink, poor lamb. Daytime b'ain't much better, neither. But night-time he wheezes somethin' terrible. Terrible! Keeps me awake, it do. Keeps me awake somethin' awful. Not had a night's proper sleep for months!

TRENT: Yes. I see. And how long have you suffered in this way, Mr Mumpkin?

MRS MUMPKIN: Tell him, Arthur!

MR MUMPKIN manages a wheeze preparatory to his answer before his wife plunges on:

MRS MUMPKIN: Nearly six months it's been now, doctor. Six months of his wheezing and coughing just like he's near his end.

TRENT: I see. Well perhaps I'd better listen to your chest.

TRENT takes a stethoscope from his desk.

MRS MUMPKIN: You wouldn't need that there contraption if you did share a bedroom with him like I do. Would he, Arthur?

Some more wheezing from ARTHUR.

MRS MUMPKIN: Wheezing, groaning, coughing, moaning. All night long. Not had a proper night's sleep for six months now, I haven't!

TRENT (*helpfully*): Well perhaps you could sleep in another room, Mrs Mumpkin.

MRS MUMPKIN: I couldn't do that! Suppose he's taken bad in the night!

TRENT: Yes, well – I'll just listen to your chest, Mr Mumpkin.

TRENT leans closer with the stethoscope.

MRS MUMPKIN: It's that grey mist what's doing for him. That's what I reckon.

TRENT hesitates.

TRENT: I'm sorry? What did you say – ?

MRS MUMPKIN: Grey mist, doctor. Nasty stuff, it is. It's on my Arthur's chest and no mistake. B'ain't it, Arthur?

There is further wheezing from MR MUMPKIN, but this time TRENT doesn't notice.

TRENT: Forgive me, Mrs Mumpkin. I have not been in practice here very long as you probably know. I am not yet entirely familiar with some of the local phrases. What exactly is - grey mist? I do not think I've seen it –

MRS MUMPKIN: Oh you don't see it! But it's there! In the air! Choking you!

TRENT: I'm still not sure I quite understand –

MRS MUMPKIN: It's not there all the time like. Don't know when it's going to come. But suddenly – there it is! Filthy, choking, nasty stuff! Choking you! Choking my poor Arthur!

TRENT is still puzzled but decides not to pursue the matter at the moment. He moves again towards MR MUMPKIN with the stethoscope.

TRENT: I see. Well, Mr Mumpkin. If you could just breathe quite normally for me –

TRENT applies the stethoscope and listens to MR MUMPKIN'S breathing. MRS MUMPKIN, though briefly silent, has leaned so far in as to be almost between them. TRENT sits back.

MRS MUMPKIN: Well, doctor?

TRENT: There's certainly some congestion there. Is your house damp at all?

MRS MUMPKIN (*defensive*): Certainly not! Dry as a bone most of the time, considering how near the stream it is and as how the garden gets a bit boggy-like when it rains a lot!

TRENT (*taking a prescription form and writing*): Yes. Well I'll give you a prescription for a tonic which should help a little. Meanwhile I'll see what I can find out about grey mist and what the likely cures are.

MRS MUMPKIN stares at him.

MRS MUMPKIN: You won't find nothing in them there medical books of yours.

TRENT: Yes well – I must say it is new to me. Though I have heard it mentioned before, I think. Don't worry, Mr Mumpkin. We'll soon have you fit and well again.

MRS MUMPKIN: There, Arthur. What d'you say to that?

MR MUMPKIN simply wheezes. TRENT hands him the prescription form which is promptly snatched from him by his wife. TRENT stands and amidst much further bustling escorts them to the door. MR MUMPKIN still wheezes.

MRS MUMPKIN: There, doctor. Just listen to that. And that's what he's like all night long! Wheezing and coughing and groaning.

TRENT (*pointedly holding open the door*): Well the tonic will help.

MRS MUMPKIN: Poor Arthur. No wonder he's never got anything to say for himself.

With further adlibbed mutterings to ARTHUR and wheezed responses they exit the room. TRENT closes the door gratefully and leans back against it, glad of the sudden silence. Then he goes to the bookshelves. He scans some medical reference titles, takes a couple down and glances at the indexes.

TRENT (*to himself*): Grey mist. Grey mist. (*Pause*) Nothing.

He puts back the final book, browses the titles again. His hand comes to rest over the photograph album. He is about to draw it from the shelf. But he stops, straightens, shivers, turns as if expecting to see somebody in the room with him. But the room is empty. Now he looks towards the window. He seems drawn over to it. As he looks out he reacts.

TRENT (*to himself*): There she is again. Standing just where she was before.

TRENT hurries to the LH door and runs out, almost colliding with JULIA who is just entering.

JULIA: Dr Trent? What is it? What's the matter?

JULIA considers following but goes to look from the window instead. KATE enters looking concerned.

KATE: What's all the commotion, miss?

JULIA: I don't know. Dr Trent rushed outside. But there's nobody out there except Corby. He seems to be looking for something. Or someone. Now he's talking to Corby. They're coming back in.

JULIA moves from the window as TRENT and CORBY are heard re-entering the house. They are talking as they enter the consulting room.

TRENT: But you must have seen her, Corby! She was standing right there on the path in front of the house.

CORBY: There were no-one, I tell you!

TRENT: She was not ten feet from you!

CORBY: I didn't see no young lady!

JULIA: Dr Trent, what is it?

TRENT: The young lady I saw from the window a couple of weeks ago, d'you remember? I thought she was a patient frightened to come in? Well she was out there again just now, exactly as before, just staring at the house. I went out to speak to her but she had gone.

JULIA: Are you sure?

TRENT: Of course I'm sure! I could see Corby weeding the flowerbeds just beyond her.

KATE: Corby?

CORBY: I saw nobody.

TRENT: You must have, man! Mr and Mrs Mumpkin had just left a minute or so earlier. I looked from the window and the young lady was there.

CORBY: I had me head down.

JULIA: Did you see the Mumpkins, Corby?

CORBY: Heard 'em, miss. Well her anyway. Didn't look up. Not my business to, like. Just got on with me diggin'.

KATE: She'll be back I expect, if she's a mind to. Whoever she is.

JULIA: Why don't you sit down, doctor? You look very pale.

TRENT: Hmm? What?

JULIA: Sit down for a minute.

TRENT: The patients.

JULIA: The Mumpkins were the last.

KATE: How about a cup of tea, sir? Tot of brandy in it.

JULIA: Yes, good idea. Please see to it, Simpkins.

KATE: Right you are, miss.

TRENT: No brandy, thankyou. But tea would be very welcome.

CORBY: Alright if I get back to me diggin' now, is it?

TRENT: You are quite certain – ?

CORBY: Told you, didn't I? Had me back to the path and me head down diggin'.

TRENT: Yes. Yes...

KATE (*to Corby*): Come on, you lummox.

KATE hustles CORBY from the room.

TRENT: Why didn't he see her?

JULIA: He's a strange person. Lost in his own thoughts a lot of the time.

TRENT: There's something...

JULIA: What?

TRENT: Something about her. That young lady, I mean. As if I know her.

JULIA: Perhaps she reminds you of someone.

TRENT: Perhaps.

JULIA: Perhaps we might go for another walk after lunch? The fresh air may do you good.

TRENT: Yes. That sounds like a good idea.

TRENT is still distracted. He holds his head, trying to remember.

TRENT: You know – she does remind me of someone. Someone I've seen recently. I just can't remember...

He sits forward suddenly. It's come back to him. He gets up and snatches the photo album from the bookshelf, sits again and rapidly turns the pages.

TRENT: In here! That's where I've seen her. There's a photograph of her in here... There!

He shows JULIA a particular photograph in the album: a young girl in Victorian clothes seated in a formal pose.

TRENT: That's her, I'm sure.

JULIA: How can it be? This photograph must be forty or fifty years old.

TRENT: It looks exactly like her.

JULIA: A relative perhaps.

TRENT pulls the photograph from the album and turns it over. For a moment he reacts oddly. He shivers.

JULIA: What is it?

TRENT: Nothing. An odd sensation for a moment. Like someone had stepped on my grave. (*Re-examining the photo*) There's no name on it. Who is she? Who are all these other people?

He flicks through the album's pages. KATE enters with two cups of tea.

KATE: Here you are, doctor. Miss.

JULIA: Thankyou, Simpkins.

KATE puts down the tea and turns to go. TRENT holds up the photo.

TRENT: Kate – would you happen to know who this lady is?

KATE is off-guard as she catches sight of the photo. Alarm shows in her face for an instant before she recovers.

KATE: No, sir. Can't say that I do.

TRENT: The photo was in this album. D'you know who these people are?

KATE: Don't know nothing about it, sir.

TRENT: Why is it in here, on the shelf with the reference books?

KATE: Always has been. Don't know why.

JULIA: Perhaps it belonged to a previous doctor?

KATE: Couldn't say, miss. (*With a breath for courage*) I'll take it away if you like, sir. If it bothers you, that is.

She goes to take the album but TRENT instinctively holds onto it.

TRENT: No, that's alright, Kate. It doesn't matter.

KATE: As you like, sir.

She executes a bobbed curtsey and leaves the room. Her manner is uneasy. TRENT considers the album for a few moments then shrugs and pushes it back into its place on the shelf.

TRENT: I feel like I've made a bit of an ass of myself over this.

JULIA: Nonsense. Too many Mrs Prymms and Mrs Mumpkins, that's all. A walk in the fresh air will soon put it right.

TRENT: Yes. Just what the doctor ordered.

They both laugh. Then for a moment there is a brief shared moment between them. JULIA finishes her tea.

JULIA: I must get on.

She leaves the room. TRENT watches her go. There is obvious affection in his gaze. Then he glances at the window, shrugs and returns to sit at his desk. He drinks his tea while he looks through some papers, occasionally making notes.

A young woman appears outside the window. She is dressed in grey, a long dress that is old-fashioned for the time. Her movements are slow and ethereal. She stares in at TRENT.

TRENT becomes aware of something behind him. He stops writing, straightens in his chair, shivers.

The figure at the window withdraws.

TRENT turns in his chair to look at the window but sees nobody. He is uneasy but shrugs off the feeling and returns to his work on the desk.

A moment passes.

The young woman comes silently through the door and stands inside the room. TRENT does not notice. She advances slowly into the room and stops midway.

TRENT is suddenly aware of someone, turns and seeing the young woman gasps loudly, standing quickly. He looks terrified.

TRENT: Verity?

MAUDE: I beg your pardon, sir?

TRENT: Are you Verity?

MAUDE: No, sir.

TRENT: Who are you?

MAUDE: Maude Prymm, sir. I'm sorry if I startled you.

TRENT: I didn't hear you come in.

MAUDE: The door was open, sir. I suppose I should have knocked. I'm looking for my aunt.

TRENT: Your aunt?

MAUDE: Yes, sir. She was coming to see you this morning.

TRENT (*light dawning*): Prymm, did you say?

MAUDE: That's right, sir. You are treating my aunt. She comes to you quite regularly. She always speaks very highly of you. She says you are going to help her with the fund-raising for the church.

TRENT (*relaxing*): Of course. Mrs Prymm. I'm afraid you've missed her. She left a little while ago. I expect she's on her way home by now.

MAUDE: Oh, I see. We arranged to meet here but she must have given me the wrong time. She gets herself so confused, poor dear. Well if I hurry I can probably catch her. I'm sorry to have troubled you, sir.

MAUDE turns to leave as TRENT thinks of something.

TRENT: Did you not see her leave yourself?

MAUDE: I beg your pardon, sir?

TRENT: Were you not standing outside earlier?

MAUDE: No, sir. I only arrived here just before I came in. As I said, my aunt told me her appointment was later than it actually was. Good day, sir.

MAUDE goes towards the door. TRENT is uneasy again, staring at the window. MAUDE turns back just inside the door.

MAUDE: Sir? When I came in you spoke a name. You said Verity. You thought I was her.

TRENT: Did I?

MAUDE: Who is Verity?

TRENT: I don't know. I... don't know.

MAUDE watches him uncertainly then smiles politely and exits. TRENT steps forward to centre-stage looking perplexed.

TRENT: I don't know.

Black out.

Scene 6

Lights come up on the main stage to represent late afternoon. Dusk is showing through the uncurtained window. TRENT and JULIA have just returned from their walk. They are both in good spirits when they enter from the LH door. There is a subtle change in their attitude to each other: they have become closer though neither has spoken of this. They are both flushed from the fresh air and their growing feelings.

Both have on outdoor coats.

TRENT: That was a most exhilarating walk. I feel so much better for it!

JULIA: I'm glad. I've worked up quite an appetite. I'll ask Simpkins to make us a pot of tea.

TRENT: Have we time? There are the evening patients - .

JULIA: They are not due for half an hour yet.

TRENT: We've been out much longer than I thought. It's getting dark. I lost track of the time.

JULIA (*softly*): So did I.

There is a brief pause. They look at each other. Then JULIA goes to the door.

JULIA: I'll see about tea. Muffins too, if there are any!

She goes from the room. TRENT stands for a moment and breathes deeply, enjoying the warm glow he feels inside. Then he takes off his coat and hangs it on the coat-stand near the door. He returns to the small table front left and clears it of one or two papers and books. Julia returns while he is doing this. She has removed her outdoor coat.

JULIA: We are in luck. There are muffins.

TRENT: Excellent.

He indicates she should sit in the armchair. He takes the upright chair facing her.

TRENT: We must have walked miles. I had no idea. That small bridge over the stream is so picturesque though. Well worth the effort to see it.

JULIA: That's the Water-Mill Bridge – though goodness knows why it's called that. There isn't a water mill anywhere near it.

TRENT: Perhaps people just like the sound of it.

JULIA: It's a good six miles from here. No wonder we are so late back.

TRENT: Yes. And if you hadn't caught your skirt on a nail on that style - .

JULIA: You shouldn't have made me climb it!

TRENT: Well, perhaps I shouldn't.

JULIA: But it was very gallant of you to help me down anyway.

TRENT: It was a pleasure.

Again the brief and slightly coy silence falls between them. KATE enters with a tray of tea things. She notices the atmosphere but says nothing about it.

KATE: Here you are, miss. Shall I pour for you?

JULIA: No thankyou, Simpkins. I'll do it.

KATE: Right you are, miss.

TRENT: Kate – we saw a bridge called the Water-Mill, but it seems there's no mill nearby.

KATE: My Lord, doctor! You have been on a hike!

TRENT: Yes. D'you have any idea why it has that name?

KATE: No, sir. None. Lot of places round here have odd names, and that's a fact. Well – (*she eyes them both with a barely-concealed smirk*) I'll leave you both to your tea.

JULIA: Thankyou, Simpkins.

KATE exits. JULIA pours tea. TRENT butters muffins.

TRENT: My only regret is that we left it so late to look at the church.

JULIA: It's very pretty in proper daylight.

TRENT: I'm sure. It just seemed somehow gloomy in the half light. Almost eerie.

JULIA: We must go back when the sun is still out. Your tea.

TRENT: Thankyou. Yes, I'd like a proper look at some of those old inscriptions. I find them fascinating.

JULIA: So I noticed. Sugar?

TRENT: Thankyou.

He spoons sugar into his teacup, thinking. Then:

TRENT: There was something odd about that churchyard, you know. A strange atmosphere. Did you notice it?

JULIA: No, I can't say I did.

TRENT: It was particularly strong by that single gravestone. You know, the one set apart from the rest and very unkempt. Do you remember it?

JULIA: I think so.

TRENT: The air grew suddenly cold as I got near it. As if – well, I don't really know...

JULIA: Perhaps it's to do with the ground level or something.

TRENT: Perhaps...

JULIA: I didn't go that close. The ground looked too muddy just there.

TRENT: I wonder whose grave it is – why it's been allowed to fall into such disrepair.

JULIA (*quickly*): You're dripping butter!

TRENT: What? Oh damn!

They laugh as he wipes melted butter from his trouser-leg with his handkerchief.

TRENT: That one was yours, but I'll do you another one.

He takes another muffin, butters it and hands it to JULIA on a plate.

JULIA: You seem to have settled in here.

TRENT: Yes, I believe I have.

JULIA: It took me a little while before I began to feel a part of the place, but I'm very glad I decided to come here now.

TRENT: You've not been here long either.

JULIA: About four months, that's all.

TRENT: Were you seconded, like me?

JULIA: No, not really. I trained in secretarial and type-writing skills originally and for a time was at a doctors' practice in Bath, doing much the sort of work that I do here.

TRENT: Bath is a lovely place.

JULIA: It is, but the work was not demanding and there were others doing the same work as me. So I changed jobs and worked at a hospital. That was more rewarding but it was busy and noisy and bustling. I really wanted somewhere quieter. I eventually saw this post advertised. I have no living family that I know of, you understand, so there was nothing to tie me down. I was fortunate enough to secure this position. It allows me independence to work to my own standards and methods.

TRENT: They are very high standards, if I may say so.

JULIA (*a little shyly but pleased*): Thankyou.

TRENT: And I suppose you'd just settled in when you had a change of doctor!

JULIA: Yes. It was a great shock when Dr Evans died. He was no great age.

TRENT: It was his heart, I understand.

JULIA: Yes, that was what finally killed him. He hadn't looked well from the time I arrived, but – it was strange and sad in a way – in the short time I worked with him I saw him age. He grew worried and almost furtive. He would never talk of it and of course it was not my place to ask, but something must have been worrying him terribly...

They are briefly silent.

TRENT (*to lighten the atmosphere again*): And now you have me.

JULIA: Yes. Now I have you.

They look at each other for a moment. TRENT seems on the point of saying something when KATE enters hurriedly, breaking the spell.

KATE: First evening patient's here. Come on!

There is sudden chaos as TRENT and JULIA jump to their feet, abandoning their tea and muffins. KATE clatters the cups and plates onto the tray and rushes it out of the room while JULIA straightens one or two items in the room and then visibly composes herself for business. As she leaves the room, TRENT gazes after her for a moment. He hears the front door being opened and rapidly wipes butter from his mouth and goes to take his seat at the desk. He notices the butter mark on his trouser-leg and scrubs at it uselessly with his handkerchief. He abandons it and laughs out loud, then composes himself and waits for the first patient to be shown in.

Black out.

Scene 7

Lights come up on the main stage.

It is around ten o'clock the same evening. The consulting room is partially lit by lamps which throw shadows here and there. TRENT is seated in the armchair, CORBY in the chair on the other side of the small table front left. They are nearing the end of a game of draughts. Glasses of beer, half empty, stand near their hands.

TRENT: You're too good at this game for me, Corby.

CORBY: Played it all me life, I has.

TRENT: I've played it myself many times too, but – .

CORBY: Natural cunning, I got, see? Up here. (*He taps his head and laughs*)

TRENT: Yes, I can see that.

> *They play in silence for a few moments then TRENT clears his throat, about to say something a little awkward.*

TRENT: I'm glad we've been able to chat, Corby. There hasn't been much opportunity since I've been here.

CORBY: Busy men, doctor, that's what we are.

TRENT: Yes. Quite. Look, I'm sorry about earlier today. When you were out digging the borders. I expect I sounded rather abrupt.

> *CORBY's hand hesitates very slightly over the draughts board then continues to move one of the pieces.*

CORBY: Don't matter.

TRENT: It was just that the young lady – whoever she is – was standing so close to you. I was sure – .

CORBY: I gets involved in me work, doctor. Regiment of soldiers could've marched up that path and I wouldn't have noticed, and that's a fact.

TRENT: It's very satisfying to be so absorbed in what you do.

CORBY: Aye, sir. That it is.

They play on in silence for a few moments.

CORBY: You and that young Miss Norbury walked out together again this afternoon, did you then?

TRENT: We're not 'walking out' together, Corby, as you put it. But she did accompany me for a stroll, yes.

CORBY: Ah yes, sir. If you says. Where'd d'you get to then?

TRENT: We looked at the countryside. There are some very pleasant views around here. Then we went onto the church, looked around the churchyard.

CORBY: Churchyard, eh?

TRENT: That's right.

CORBY: Bit morbid, b'ain't it?

TRENT: I don't know. I've always been fascinated by gravestone inscriptions. All those lives that have been and gone. You can sometimes guess at what the person must have been like just by the way the inscription is worded. And by the state of the grave. Whether it's kept tended or not.

CORBY: The dead are dead in my book. And best left that way. Don't do no good poking around with them, that's what I say.

TRENT: Yes, well... I must admit that particular churchyard had got an atmosphere to it, something slightly chilling.

CORBY: They're all like that, if you asks me.

TRENT: We did get there rather later than we'd intended. The sun had gone. It was starting to get chilly and the light was gloomy. That probably had a lot to do with it.

A few more moments of silent play. The game is nearing its end.

TRENT: There was one grave I noticed there in particular. It was set apart from the others and was especially badly tended. The grass had grown wild around it and there was so much moss and lichen on the stone the inscription was difficult to read.

CORBY doesn't reply. He seems intent on the game.

TRENT: The atmosphere I spoke of seemed particularly strong just there. The air was colder. I could just about make out the name on the stone. It looked like – .

CORBY moves pieces with a triumphant flourish, winning the game.

CORBY: That's you seen to, doctor!

TRENT: Oh! Well done, Corby.

CORBY: Another game?

TRENT glances towards the grandfather clock which lies in deeper shadow in the corner of the room. CORBY drains his beer glass.

TRENT: It's getting late, and you're too good for me anyway. Look, I was telling you about this gravestone – .

CORBY: Best leave the dead to themselves if you ask me, and put your efforts into the living. You should know that more than most in your job, doctor.

TRENT: Yes. I suppose that's true.

CORBY: There's enough that's strange and unexplained around these parts already without going looking for more of it.

TRENT: What d'you mean?

CORBY: You been to the old public house since you been here?

TRENT: The inn on that sharp bend in the lane, you mean?

CORBY: That's the one.

TRENT: No I haven't been inside. I've passed it a few times. It's got a strange sort of name, I seem to remember...

CORBY: Aye, it has that. The Dead Man's Turning.

TRENT: Yes that's it! I don't think I've ever come across an inn with such a name before.

CORBY: Don't suppose you has, sir.

TRENT: How did it – ?

CORBY: Come by the name? Well I'll tell you the tale, doctor. But I'm going to need a bit more of this if I do.

He picks up his empty glass, reaches down and picks up a large jug of ale from the floor and refills his glass.

CORBY: You, doctor?

TRENT: Just half a glass.

CORBY pours beer into TRENT's glass then settles himself more comfortably. TRENT does the same.

CORBY: T'were like this, see. Many many years ago there were a gibbet stood on the other side of the road to where the inn is now, right on that little raised bit of land, just where the road makes its turn.

TRENT: Just on the sharp bend?

CORBY: Aye. Just there. Well the hangings used attract the crowds, folk bein' what folk are like, and the crowds got thirsty, which is how the inn came to be, see. Some of the worst murderers and thieves in the county met their end out there at the end of the rope. Big event, it were, the public hangin', in those days. But – like all good things – it come to an end. (*He grins*) The public hangin's stopped but the old gibbet, 'e stood out there for a good many more years til in the end 'e got taken away or 'e fell down, just dependin' on which version you hear.

CORBY shifts his position a little and drinks, as if his story is finished. TRENT is slightly confused.

TRENT: And that's why the inn got its name - ?

CORBY: Well, not quite, doctor, no. Not quite. See there's a bit more to it than that. After the hangin's stopped folk started to say they'd seen things out there, on the road near where the old gibbet had stood, like, in the dead of night.

TRENT: Seen things?

CORBY: Figures standin' in the road, like, when there weren't nobody there.

TRENT: It's a very dark stretch just there. Perhaps it was the shadow of a tree.

CORBY: Perhaps. But you can't have all them violent deaths in one spot without it leavin' some mark on the land, now can you?

TRENT: Well, I suppose not, but...

CORBY: Anyway, one of these folk was Lord Henry. Oh he weren't a lord really, just got called that by the folk round here 'cos he were the magistrate and squire and lived in the big house on the far side of the hill. Magistratin' were in his family, you might say. His father'd been magistrate, and his father, and his... all the way back to when the old gibbet was still used for the public hangins'. (*Pause*) Well. Late one night Lord Henry were headin' home from some meetin' and dinner. He had his own carriage, bein' as how 'e were gentry, like. Nice two-seater, it were, with one horse to pull it. He had the canopy up 'cos this were in wintertime and the night air were cold. Lord Henry had to come that way to get to his house, see. Well, he come to the bend and started round it. As the carriage drew level with where the old gibbet had been Lord Henry saw a figure stood in the road ahead, right in his way. He couldn't see who the figure were, just that he stood somehow crooked, head bent to one side, like. Now old Lord Henry weren't a man to suffer fools gladly and he yelled at the figure to get out of his blasted way. But just

then the horse took fright and reared in the trestles. Took
Lord Henry all his skill and strength to get the carriage under
control and calm the horse. And when he had, the figure had
gone from the road like it were never there, and Henry trotted
on. But he'd only gone another fifty yards or so when he felt
an icy cold down his left side such as he'd never known
before. He looked round to see what were causing it – and
there were the figure sat next to him in the carriage, head still
bent over where the rope had once broke the neck, eyes
bulging and the tongue all hung out. When Lord Henry got
home later that night he seemed to have aged twenty years.
They say he lay in bed several days like he had the deliriums,
and chanted the story over and over again. When he died a
few days after the doctor said it were his heart had given out.
And you know what, Dr Trent... I reckon it were. He were
the last of his family to do magistratin' round here.

*TRENT seems mesmerised by the story. CORBY drinks off the
rest of his beer.*

TRENT: Is this story true?

CORBY: Who can say? It's been told so many times folk take it as
      truth. And it's a strange place, that corner by the inn, if you
      happens to be there late at night. There's a lot of tales like
      that around here, doctor. Best to take no notice of them, is
      my advice.

CORBY stands.

CORBY: It's late. I'll be off to me bed.

TRENT: Yes. Thank you for your company this evening.

CORBY: Just think on what I said. There's a lot of superstitious
      folk round here and they talk superstitious talk. Don't be
      listening to it. Good night.

TRENT: Good night, Corby.

CORBY takes his glass and the beer jug and exits the room. TRENT remains seated for a few moments, lost in thought. He drains his beer and packs up the draughts board. He returns it to a drawer then stands for a moment in the centre of the room. The wind has got up during the course of CORBY's story. It moans eerily outside. TRENT goes over to the bookshelves and after a moment's search selects a volume entitled 'Local Folklore'. He flicks though it superficially then returns with it to the armchair and sits again. He begins to study the book. He yawns deeply, settles back in the armchair more comfortably and soon his head begins to nod. The book lays open on his knees as he falls into a deep sleep.

The stage is absolutely still for a few moments. There is just the sound of the low moaning wind. Then a soft whimpering female cry is heard, repeated several times: it is the same voice Trent heard earlier – VERITY'S voice.

TRENT stirs in the armchair, disturbed in his sleep, but does not wake.

The voice whimpers again, louder now: there is great distress in it.

TRENT stirs again restlessly. After a moment more of silence, VERITY'S voice is heard: it is a plaintive sound and seems to come from no particular direction:

VERITY (*off*): Help me. Please help me.

The sound of the wind has grown a little stronger. TRENT murmurs restlessly in his sleep, shifting uneasily in the chair.

VERITY (*off - louder*): Help me please. Help me.

TRENT wakes suddenly with a start. He sits up in the chair. The book falls from his knees to the floor with a loud clatter. He stares straight ahead as if in sudden horror.

TRENT: Verity Mandrake!

He gets to his feet. He is a little unsteady. He seems very afraid. He stares around the semi-darkened room as if certain he is not alone. He goes unsteadily to the desk and leans on it, still staring around the room.

TRENT (*to himself as if having discovered something*): Verity Mandrake.

Now he stares towards the closed curtains at the window. He goes towards them slowly as if still in a state of trance. He takes hold of the left-hand curtain and pulls it open suddenly.

VERITY stands right outside the window, staring in at him. She is starkly lighted from below. She wears the grey dress. Her face is pallid and hollow. Her expression is terrifying.

A long piercing female scream is heard at the same moment VERITY is revealed.

TRENT lurches backwards with a cry of terror, putting his hands to his face.

Black out.

CURTAIN

ACT 2:

Scene 1

When the curtain rises the main stage remains in semi-darkness. A spotlight illuminates the NARRATOR who is on the arm of the easy chair DL.

NARRATOR: As I understand the story, Dr Trent made no mention to anyone of what he had seen at the window that night. Well not just then anyway. It is possible that by the next morning – in the cold light of day, as the saying goes – he had grown to doubt the evidence of his own eyes. He had been sleeping in the chair – this chair – and had woken suddenly. He had been drinking after a tiring day. The wind was moaning outside. The story he had been told by Corby was still fresh in his mind. Perhaps, after all, it had been in his imagination – a sort of waking dream. Or simply just that – a dream. Perhaps he had not actually woken at that moment at all.

All these things he must have told himself the next morning as he tried to rationalise the incident of the night before. But a name stayed with him. Verity Mandrake. He felt sure he had not dreamed that.

Several days passed without further event, but Dr Trent did not forget. He returned to the churchyard on one of these days, alone this time, in the early afternoon while the sun was still bright. Whatever sensations or forebodings he might have felt at being there, he went to that single gravestone he had noticed before, and this time he examined it closely.

Spotlight fades on the NARRATOR, who exits the stage.

Lights come up on the main stage. It is afternoon. JULIA is tidying and sorting papers on Trent's desk. She carries one or two to the filing cabinet L and puts them away. She returns to the desk and sorts more papers, then hesitates over a sheet of paper that has been partially hidden. She examines it: on it is written the name Verity Mandrake again and again in Trent's handwriting. JULIA is puzzled.

JULIA (*to herself*): Verity Mandrake. Written again and again. Dr Trent...?

Footsteps are heard in the corridor. JULIA slips the sheet of paper back on the desk out of sight as KATE enters from the LH door. She carries a duster.

KATE: Sorry, miss. Didn't realise you was in here, like. Just come to tidy round.

JULIA: I'm filing things away.

KATE: I'll come back later then. When you've finished. (*She turns to go.*)

JULIA: Does Dr Trent have a patient called Verity Mandrake?

KATE tenses visibly but JULIA does not notice. KATE hesitates for a moment.

KATE: Not that I know to, miss. Don't know the names of all his patients mind.

JULIA: Well I suppose I can look in the patients' records.

KATE: Yes, miss. I'll get on. Come back later when you've finished.

JULIA: Thankyou.

KATE looks uneasy as she exits. JULIA takes out the sheet of paper again bearing Verity's name and studies it for a moment more, then goes over to the filing cabinet. She studies the drawers curiously, wondering where to start.

JULIA (*to herself*): Mandrake – Mandrake.

She is on the point of opening a drawer when she hears footsteps on the path outside. She goes to the window and looks out.

JULIA: Dr Trent.

She looks guiltily at the sheet of paper then quickly returns it to the desk where she found it and gathers up some further papers, as if in the process of sorting them.

TRENT enters wearing his overcoat and carrying his doctor's bag. He looks preoccupied, a little drawn.

JULIA: Dr Trent. I was taking the opportunity to file away some papers.

TRENT: What? Oh yes. I'm afraid I'm not very methodical when it comes to paperwork.

He removes his coat, hangs it up and goes to the window to glance out. JULIA watches him with some concern. As he turns back she disguises her anxiety with a smile.

JULIA: Well, I can do this later if you need to use your desk.

TRENT: No – no, that's fine. Please carry on. I'll sit here.

He goes to the armchair and sits, putting the doctor's bag on the small table. JULIA shuffles the papers she is holding then takes them to file in the cabinet. After a moment:

JULIA: Have you been walking?

TRENT: Yes.

JULIA: It's a fine day.

TRENT: Yes, it is. I had to call at Drifters Farm on the other side of the village. Farmer's young lad with stomach ache. Nothing serious. On the way back I stopped at the inn. You know – the one with the odd name – The Dead Man's Turning.

JULIA: Lunchtime drinking, doctor?

TRENT: Oh I didn't go inside. I wanted to look at the inn. Well the ground opposite actually. Have you heard the story about it, about that stretch of road outside the inn?

JULIA: I don't think so.

TRENT: Corby told me about it. It is supposed to be haunted. Things have been seen there. I wanted to look for myself. I'm never sure with Corby if he is having a secret joke at my expense.

JULIA: He is an odd man. What did he tell you?

TRENT: He said that public hangings used to take place there years ago, right on the sharp corner where the inn stands now. Figures are said to have appeared to travellers in the road there in the dead of night – the tortured spirits of the gallows victims, it is said.

JULIA: Sounds like an old wives' tale to me. The locals are a superstitious lot I've found.

TRENT: Well I didn't see anything anyway. But then I was there in the middle of the afternoon in broad daylight, so I suppose I wouldn't. Even so, there is something just there. A slight coldness... (*A pause, then:*) Do you – do you believe in ghosts, Miss Norbury?

She pauses briefly with the filing, considers, then answers with light amusement:

JULIA: It's something I've never really thought about. I don't think so, no. Do you?

TRENT (*quickly*): No... That is, no I never have. And yet since I've been here – .

JULIA: What?

TRENT: I don't know. The atmosphere of this place – this area – is strange sometimes. It can cause the imagination to run away. (*Pause*) I went on to the churchyard afterwards. Looked around. Looked at that strange desolated gravestone again. I don't know why. Something sort of draws me to it, almost against my will. The air around it was cold again. Just like on that day before when we visited it.

He pauses and seems to shiver. JULIA looks concerned. She leaves the filing and comes to sit opposite him.

JULIA: Are you alright?

TRENT: Yes. Well – that is – a strange thing happened.

JULIA: On your own in that gloomy churchyard, I'm not surprised.

TRENT: Yes well that's the thing. I wasn't on my own. There was a child there. A young girl of perhaps nine or ten. She was perched on one of the tombstones when I arrived, sketching. She didn't appear to notice me at first. I didn't wish to disturb her so I just wandered about a bit, went and looked at the isolated grave as I told you. But after a while I felt she was watching me. So I went over to her – said hello and that it was a pleasant day. She looked back at me but didn't answer. Then I realised she was looking past me, towards that particular grave, I thought – as if she could see someone standing there. I looked around instinctively – but of course there was nobody. I asked her then what she was drawing so earnestly and did she mind if I looked...

TRENT falters.

JULIA: Yes?

TRENT: She leapt down from the tombstone as if terrified and ran off through the churchyard as if all the hounds from hell were chasing her. I called out that I was sorry if I'd frightened her – that I hadn't meant to. But she was gone.

JULIA: Her mother has probably warned her about talking to strangers, that's all.

TRENT: Perhaps. It isn't that really. Her behaviour seemed odd, I admit. But –

JULIA: What?

TRENT: She left her drawing behind.

JULIA: If she was frightened – .

> *TRENT hesitates. Then he opens the doctor's bag which stands on the small table. He pulls out a folded sheet of paper. For a moment he seems reluctant to unfold it. Finally he does so, handing it to JULIA. She stares at it. It is a childish sketch of an unkempt gravestone. Two figures have been drawn standing one on either side of the grave. One is a man holding a small bag. The other is a woman in a ground-length grey dress.*

TRENT: You see what she had drawn?

JULIA: It's a gravestone with a man standing on one side of it and a woman standing on the other.

TRENT: The man is holding a small bag, isn't he? A small bag – like this one (*indicating his doctor's bag*)

JULIA: Well that's natural, I suppose. She saw you in the churchyard and put you into her picture.

TRENT: Then who is the other figure? Who is the woman?

JULIA: The imaginings of a young child, probably. She drew in a friend for you.

TRENT: Yes. Perhaps.

JULIA: Who do you think it is?

TRENT (*hesitant*): I'm not sure. It sounds ridiculous. But I thought –

JULIA: Yes?

TRENT: I thought it was supposed to be the woman buried in that grave.

JULIA: Perhaps it is. A young girl's imagination afterall...

TRENT: Yes. Imagination, as you say. That's one of the few drawbacks to being in a place like this, I suppose. The superstitions of the locals, as you mentioned – the stories you hear. The strange sense of an atmosphere – which may be imagined or may not be. I'm not a superstitious man. At least I didn't think I was. As a doctor you have to have a practical mind, as you must know. (*Pause*) You asked me just now if I believed in ghosts. Well if you'd asked me two months ago I'd have laughed the question off as utter nonsense. But now –

He shrugs, shifts in his seat. His mood lightens a little, though this could be artificial.

TRENT: The power of suggestion – the influence of one's surroundings on the workings of the mind. Now that is more in my line. And I suppose that's what's happening here. You see, after I left the churchyard I felt strangely unnerved by what had happened. That young girl and her drawing. The way she had looked beyond me towards that decrepit grave. I suppose I should have left the sketch where it was but somehow I felt compelled to take it with me. That figure she had drawn – the woman – made me think of someone, but I couldn't bring it to mind who it was. Anyway I cut across the fields to get back here quickly rather than go the long way around by the lane – you know, it's the way that takes you through the woods. The path there is almost non-existent and the trees come in very close in places. I was halfway along when it came to me – who the girl's drawing made me think of.

JULIA: Who?

TRENT: You remember that I saw a young lady outside here a couple of times – a patient I thought was frightened to come in? Well that's who the sketch reminded me of.

JULIA looks at the drawing again then smiles.

JULIA: It's a child's sketch – and not a very good one. This figure could be anyone.

TRENT: I know. It's stupid, isn't it? That's what I mean about the power of suggestion over the logic of the mind.

JULIA: It's the only explanation.

TRENT: Yes it is. And yet – . I'm afraid this will sound very
  idiotic – .

JULIA: What?

TRENT: As I went further into the trees I began to feel someone
  was walking behind me. I couldn't hear anyone. I just sensed
  it. I stopped a couple of times and looked back – but of
  course there was nobody there. I went on a little farther – and
  suddenly the sensation was much stronger. It brought me to a
  dead stop. I looked back again. And for a moment I thought –
  (*pause*)

JULIA: What?

TRENT: For a moment I thought I saw that young lady standing
  just off the path amidst the trees watching me. (*Pause*) It
  gave me quite a start. I looked away involuntarily and when I
  looked again I couldn't see her. I went on quickly. I wanted
  to get out of the trees. The air had seemed to turn cold and
  hostile suddenly. I was glad when I got back on the road. Of
  course then – in the open again – I just felt a bit of an ass and
  doubted I'd seen anything at all.

JULIA: Your mind was playing tricks, I'm sure.

TRENT: It's very dark in those trees. And as I saw her she was
  dressed in dark grey – very hard to distinguish amongst all
  the shadows. Yet for those few seconds she seemed utterly
  real. And the strange thing was that I suddenly realised that I
  knew her name.

JULIA: Her name?

TRENT: In the churchyard earlier I managed to read the name on
  that isolated grave. I had to pull away some of the lichen and
  moss first but in the better light I could make it out.

JULIA (*warily*): What name was it?

TRENT: Verity Mandrake.

*JULIA reacts, remembering the names on the sheet of paper, but
quickly hides her reaction from TRENT.*

TRENT: That's who I think the young girl has drawn in her
    picture.

*JULIA looks again at the drawing. TRENT gets to his feet and
goes over to the desk. He takes from a drawer the photograph of
the girl that had been in the photo album.*

TRENT: Let me show you something else.

*JULIA rises and meets TRENT in the centre of the room. She
still holds the drawing. He shows her the photo.*

TRENT: Look at this. It's the photograph I found in that old album
    from the bookshelf. D'you remember? The anonymous girl in
    Victorian dress.

JULIA: Yes, but – .

TRENT: I think this is her. Verity Mandrake.

*JULIA takes the photo from him. She compares it to the
drawing.*

JULIA: It's possible, I suppose.

TRENT: I'm certain of it.

JULIA: Well perhaps. If she was a local person, connected in some
    way to whoever lived here at the time, there's no reason why
    her photograph shouldn't be in that album.

TRENT: That's right.

JULIA: But there's no reason to suppose it's the same person in
    this drawing. The sketch could be of anyone.

TRENT: I'm sure it's her.

JULIA (*doubtful*): Well...

TRENT goes to the window and looks out.

TRENT: That young lady I've seen standing out there - .

JULIA: I don't know. She could be a relation – a descendant. A grand-daughter, maybe?

TRENT returns to JULIA's side. He takes the photo and the drawing from her, studying them.

TRENT: I need to find out who she is – the girl I've seen out there. Somebody must know her. And I need to find out who this woman in the photo is – and what became of her.

JULIA: Really, d'you think that's wise? It might be best left alone.

TRENT takes a pace forward.

TRENT (*almost to himself*): Who was Verity Mandrake? I have to know.

Blackout.

Scene 2

Spotlight comes up on the NARRATOR. He stands by the armchair.

NARRATOR: And so Dr Trent was determined to find out whatever he could. It is unlikely, had anyone - other than Julia Norbury - realised what he was doing, that they could have stopped him anyway, such was his growing obsession with the matter. And if they had – would it have made any difference in the end? Personally, I don't think it would.

Spotlight fades and the NARRATOR exits. Lights on main stage come up. It is late in the evening – about ten o'clock. The consulting room is partially lit by several lamps, including the one at the desk at which TRENT sits. The curtains at the window are not drawn. It is dark outside. TRENT has several books opened on his desk. He also has the photograph of Verity and the child's drawing. He puts down the volume he has been reading with a long sigh of frustration.

TRENT (*to himself*): Nothing! No mention at all in any of these! She must have been a local person to be buried in the churchyard. So she must have been a patient here surely. So why is there no mention of her? There must be something somewhere!

He sits back, thinking.

TRENT: Verity Mandrake... Verity Mandrake....

Outside the window, just visible as a dark silhouette, the figure of VERITY steps into view slowly. She stands close to the window and faces directly towards TRENT at the desk. She stands utterly still. TRENT shivers, but is otherwise unaware of this. He has an idea.

TRENT: The church must have records! Burial records!

He sits forward again, picks up the photo and studies it.

TRENT: This must have been taken fifty or sixty years ago, so – .

He puts down the photo and returns to the volumes on the desk, picking them up one after another.

TRENT: There's a volume missing! There's a gap in the dates!

He is on the point of getting up when he seems suddenly aware of VERITY. He does not turn but sits straight, gasps, shivers. VERITY speaks but her voice does not seem to come from the figure at the window. We cannot see her talking.

VERITY (*off*): Help me. Please. Help me.

TRENT turns suddenly. He now sees the figure. He catches his breath. Slowly he gets to his feet. He believes it to be the patient who is frightened to come in. The lighting outside the window is such that VERITY is very indistinct – no more than a shadowy figure.

TRENT (*to himself breathlessly*): It's her. Why has she come so late?

He advances slowly towards the window, wary of frightening her.

TRENT (*to Verity*): It's alright. Don't be afraid. Don't be frightened. Do you want to see me? Do you want to see a doctor?

*TRENT is nearing the window when CORBY's voice is heard off
– a sudden bellowed, blood-curdling cry of utter agony. TRENT
is startled. He looks towards the door then back to the window.*

TRENT: God in heaven! What was that? (*to VERITY*): Everything's
alright! Stay where you are!

*TRENT runs out of the door L to find out what has happened. As
he does so, VERITY withdraws from sight slowly. There is a
sound of commotion off: the voices of KATE, JULIA and TRENT
can be heard – and of CORBY moaning in agony. After a few
moments they all re-enter the consulting room. TRENT supports
CORBY with help from KATE. JULIA follows. CORBY's left
sleeve is rolled up. His forearm is covered in blood. He is in
agony and looks ready to pass out. They get him into Trent's
chair at the desk, talking rapidly:*

TRENT: Help me get him into the chair. What happened?

KATE: He were choppin' sticks for the fire.

JULIA: It looks awful.

KATE: Told him it were too dark. But he wouldn't listen.

TRENT: I'll need hot water.

KATE: Great lummox! Chopped hisself!

TRENT: Hot water, Kate! Now!

KATE: Yes, sir.

KATE leaves quickly for the water.

TRENT (*to JULIA*): I need antiseptic and bandages.

JULIA goes to fetch the things. CORBY is moaning.

TRENT: It's alright, Corby. Probably far worse than it looks.

CORBY: It were the mist. Couldn't see.

JULIA (*returning*): Here you are.

CORBY: I need more light.

JULIA: Alright.

CORBY: Come down all around me. Sudden like. Couldn't see.

TRENT: Just keep still, Corby.

> *JULIA switches on the main room light and returns to the desk. TRENT is examining the wound.*

JULIA: How bad is it?

TRENT: I can't tell until I can wash some of this blood away.

CORBY: Couldn't see. The mist were everywhere. Grey mist, just like they talk of. Come down all sudden like.

JULIA: What's he saying? What do you mean, Corby?

CORBY: The grey mist, it were.

JULIA: Grey mist?

TRENT (*realising*): Grey mist? Corby! What are you saying? What grey mist?

> *KATE re-enters with a bowl of water. She hears the conversation, intervening quickly as she brings the bowl to the desk.*

KATE: He don't know what he's saying. He's delirious. Daft lummox!

> *TRENT begins to bathe the wound, apply antiseptic and bandages. Concentrating on this, he has briefly forgotten the reference to grey mist.*

TRENT: It doesn't look too bad. It's deep but a clean cut.

KATE: Told you not to go choppin' sticks in the dark.

TRENT: Get the bandages ready.

KATE: Great lummox!

TRENT: Kate! Bandages!

KATE: Yes, sir.

JULIA is cutting strips of bandage and cotton-wool wadding. She hands them to KATE. TRENT takes them and begins to dress the wound.

TRENT: Get this water out of the way.

JULIA: I'll do it.

JULIA takes the bowl of blood-coloured water from the room. TRENT ties bandages around the wound on CORBY's forearm.

TRENT: This is going to hurt for a few days, Corby. But I think you'll live. Fortunately you didn't hit an artery.

KATE: More's the pity!

TRENT: With luck the antiseptic will stop any infection. God knows what the blade of that axe of yours has got on it.

CORBY: If I'da known I were goin' to chop me arm I'd have used a clean one.

KATE: He's feeling better.

TRENT: Good. You still look pale.

CORBY: Shock, that is. A drop of brandy's what I need now. B'ain't that what you'd prescribe, doctor? For bad shock? A good dose of brandy?

TRENT: Yes, Corby. I think that's probably a good idea.

TRENT has completed the dressing and stands up. To KATE:

TRENT: Take him through to the scullery and give him some brandy. Not too much though. (*To CORBY:*) Can you stand? Can you manage to walk?

CORBY: I'll manage.

KATE: If there's brandy involved, he'll manage.

CORBY gets to his feet, wincing. He seems a bit unsteady, but waves away assistance. KATE hovers close as he moves towards the door.

CORBY: Stop fussing me, woman! I'm alright!

KATE: Next time aim for your neck! Daft lummox!

They meet JULIA in the doorway. She steps to one side to let them through. There is more chuntering from CORBY and KATE as they exit. TRENT has resumed his seat, relieved that the emergency is over. JULIA comes over to him.

TRENT: What a drama!

JULIA: Will he be alright?

TRENT: Yes, I think so. So long as the wound doesn't get infected. I'll need to check it regularly.

JULIA: I wonder how he came to be so careless?

TRENT: He said he was chopping wood when – (*suddenly remembering Verity*) The young lady!

JULIA: What?

TRENT gets up and goes quickly to the window and looks out.

TRENT: The young lady! The frightened patient! She was outside when this happened! I asked her to wait – .

TRENT hurries from the room. The sound of the front door opening is heard. JULIA goes to the window and peers out into the darkness until TRENT returns a few moments later.

TRENT: No sign of her. She's gone.

JULIA: I don't understand.

TRENT: I was busy at the desk and when I looked up she was at the window, looking in. That same young lady I've seen standing on the path outside on previous occasions. I heard her voice. She asked me to help her. I called to her, told her she had nothing to fear – and that's when I heard Corby's yell. In the excitement I forgot she was there. Now she's gone again. The panic must have frightened her off. Damn it!

JULIA: I'm sure she'll come back.

TRENT: I was looking through these old practice record books. Trying to find a reference to a Verity Mandrake. I thought she might once have been a patient here. Did you know one of the volumes is missing?

JULIA: Missing? Are you sure?

TRENT: The one for 1888.

JULIA: I've rarely had cause to consult them.

TRENT: And what did Corby mean about a grey mist coming down around him?

JULIA: I don't know. I thought he was rambling because of the shock.

TRENT: I've heard him mention it before. Someone else too... The Mumpkins talked of it. Well, she did anyway.

JULIA: Perhaps it's a local expression.

TRENT: It was as though he blamed the mist for his accident.

JULIA: I suspect he'd already had a drink or two before he went out to chop wood. I could smell the alcohol on him. It's more likely that that is the cause of his accident.

TRENT: There are too many unanswered questions.

TRENT makes a decisive move as if to leave the room, but JULIA catches his hand instinctively. TRENT stops and looks at her. There is suddenly an air of intimacy between them.

JULIA: You won't find the answer to any of them tonight.

TRENT: No. You're right. There have been too many shocks already this evening.

He gently touches her hand which rests on his.

TRENT: I expect you think I'm a supreme dramatist, don't you? Hardly what you'd expect from a solid reliable country practitioner.

JULIA (*softy*): I think you are a very good doctor who is very keen to do his job properly and is now getting tired and anxious.

TRENT: I think you understand me too well.

There is a moment between them. They stand close. TRENT leans towards her and kisses her briefly and gently. They stand for a moment more, then each becomes a little awkward. TRENT steps away, letting go of her hand.

TRENT: Well. Tomorrow I shall go back to the church and speak to the vicar, ask if I can look at the burial record for that isolated grave.

JULIA: You're very determined, aren't you?

TRENT: I must know about Verity Mandrake.

JULIA: Then I'll go with you.

A pause. They look at each other, then away. JULIA moves to the door.

JULIA: It's late. We both need rest.

TRENT: Thankyou, Julia. Good night.

JULIA: Good night.

She exits the room. TRENT remains standing in the room's centre. He breathes a long sigh. There is a mixture of emotions in his expression. He looks at the window then goes over and pulls the curtains. He goes to the lamp on the desk and switches it off. Simultaneously -

Blackout.

Scene 3

Lights come up on main stage. It is late afternoon the following day. KATE and CORBY are together in the consulting room. They are in the middle of a heated discussion. CORBY's arm is now in a sling.

KATE: You need to watch your mouth, you great lummox!

CORBY: I couldn't think what I were saying, could I?

KATE: That were obvious!

CORBY: I'd just sliced me arm open, woman! Anyhow, I don't think they noticed.

KATE: Well just watch your talk of grey mist next time.

CORBY: He'll find out soon enough anyway, like as not.

KATE: You don't know that! Perhaps he won't. Maybe things'll be different this time.

CORBY: Don't talk soft, woman. You know how it'll be. You know how it is always is – how it'll always be.

KATE: I just thought that – .

CORBY: Look, there b'ain't nothing can be done – and you knows it! That's just the way it is.

There comes the sound of the front door opening and voices off – TRENT and JULIA.

CORBY: Hush now, woman! They're back!

TRENT enters wearing outdoor clothes. He takes off his overcoat and hangs it on the coat-stand.

KATE: Nice walk, sir?

TRENT: Yes. Thankyou.

KATE: We were just tidying around in here.

TRENT: Good. How's the arm, Corby?

CORBY: S'alright.

TRENT: I'd better take a look at it.

CORBY: No need. S'alright.

TRENT: Really I think I should. You don't want to risk an infection in the wound.

KATE: Do what the doctor says, Corby.

CORBY: If you says so.

KATE: I'll leave you to it. (*She starts for the door.*)

TRENT: Oh, just a moment. There's something I wanted to ask you both.

KATE turns. She exchanges a very brief warning look with CORBY.

TRENT: I was looking through the old practice records last evening. One of them seems to be missing. Would either of you know where it might be?

KATE (*quickly*): No good asking us, doctor. We neither of us have ever had any business with them records. That's right, b'ain't it, Corby?

CORBY shrugs in agreement.

TRENT (*not entirely convinced*): I see. Well thank you, anyway. It's a volume similar to those – dated 1888. If you do happen to see it lying around somewhere please bring it to me.

KATE: Very good, sir.

KATE executes a short curtsey and exits. TRENT motions CORBY to the patient's chair and himself sits at the desk. CORBY sits.

TRENT: Now then. Let's take a look at this injury.

They are both silent for a moment while TRENT carefully removes the sling and bandage. CORBY seems uneasy.

CORBY: You alright, doctor? You look tired, washed out.

TRENT: Probably the excitement of last night. I haven't been sleeping too well recently.

CORBY: Bad dreams, is it? Nightmares? Well, we all gets those.

TRENT: Yes.

CORBY: B'ain't nothing to worry about though.

TRENT: I'm sure not. (*Indicating the wound*) That doesn't look too bad. You were lucky.

CORBY: Always lucky, me. Born under a lucky star, I were.

TRENT: I envy you.

TRENT is now replacing the bandage. There is a moment's silence, then:

TRENT: What is the grey mist?

CORBY (*flinching*): What?

TRENT: Keep still. The grey mist. You were saying something about it when we brought you in here last night.

CORBY (*wary*): Were I?

TRENT: You said a grey mist had come down all around you suddenly.

CORBY: I were in shock. Didn't know what I were saying. Weren't making any sense.

TRENT: That's understandable. But you've mentioned it before, I think.

CORBY: People talk soft round here sometimes. Don't want to take no notice of most of what they say. Foolish talk, it be. Just foolish talk. You finished?

TRENT: Yes.

CORBY stands up, eager to avoid more questions.

TRENT: I'll look at the wound again tomorrow.

CORBY: If you says so. Must get on now. Things to attend to.

CORBY exits. TRENT is thoughtful as he clears away after the brief examination. JULIA enters the room. She has already removed her outdoor coat. She carries tea things on a tray which she puts on the small table DL.

JULIA: Here we are. Tea and muffins.

TRENT: Lovely. You spoil me.

JULIA smiles at his remark. He comes over to her while she is pouring tea. He sits but seems distracted.

TRENT: There's something about those two.

JULIA: Simpkins and Corby?

TRENT: I always feel they're keeping something back. I asked them about the missing volume of medical records. They said they knew nothing – but – I don't know – it was as if a signal went between them.

JULIA: They're country folk. Maybe they thought you were blaming them for its loss.

TRENT: Perhaps. I don't know. Maybe I imagined it. I also asked Corby what he'd meant about the grey mist last night but he said he didn't remember what he was saying.

JULIA: Well I'm not surprised after what he'd just done to himself.

TRENT: He flinched though when I asked him. As if the question frightened him.

JULIA: It was probably just his arm. Here's your tea.

*She hands him the cup and saucer. He takes it then studies her
with a mixture of admiration and amusement. After a moment
JULIA notices. She looks slightly embarrassed.*

JULIA: What is it?

TRENT: I was just thinking how wonderfully practical you are.

JULIA: Oh I don't know about that.

TRENT: Whenever I mention my suspicions and anxieties – you
always have a rational explanation for me. I think, you know,
that if you weren't here I'd be starting to go just a little mad
by now.

JULIA: Then it's a good thing I am here. Now drink your tea
before it gets cold.

TRENT: I think it's a good thing you're here too. A very good
thing.

JULIA smiles again and they drink in silence for a moment.

TRENT: What did you make of our visit to the church this
afternoon? Do you have a rational explanation for that?

JULIA: No, I don't. The vicar seemed – well – frightened, I
thought.

TRENT: Yes. That was my impression too.

JULIA: He was keen enough at first.

TRENT: He thought he'd got two new parishioners – thought Mrs
Prymm had done her job! His remarks about the state of the
church roof and the charity events he had in mind to raise
money for its repair were hardly subtle. Until I mentioned
Verity Mandrake's grave. Then he just seemed to clam up.

JULIA: He almost physically backed away.

TRENT: Did you notice how pale he went when I asked about the
burial register?

JULIA: He said it had been damaged through dampness and been
sent away for repair.

TRENT: I'm not sure I believe that. But – why should a man of the cloth tell such a lie?

JULIA: He's frightened of something.

TRENT: I looked at that grave again while you were saying goodbye to the vicar. This time I could just distinguish the dates on it. Verity Mandrake died in 1888. The same year as the missing medical register.

Blackout

Scene 4

Lights come up on the main stage. It is the next morning.

MR AND MRS MUMPKIN have returned. As before, MRS MUMPKIN has drawn the extra chair up very close so that she has almost inserted herself between TRENT in his chair and MR MUMPKIN in the patient's chair. The consultation has been in progess for some time and it is clear that MRS MUMPKIN has been interjecting on her husband's behalf on a regular basis. TRENT is attempting to keep his patience.

TRENT: And you say the breathlessness has got worse in the last day or so, Mr Mumpkin?

MRS MUMPKIN: Worse than it's ever been, doctor, and that's the truth. Specially last evening. Could hardly utter a word, poor lamb. Never knew him so quiet.

TRENT: Do you have any pains, Mr Mumpkin?

MRS MUMPKIN: Pains? Course he got pains! He has pains all the time something shocking, he do. All the time he has –

TRENT (*patient but firm*): Mrs Mumpkin, I am going to need a bowl of hot water in a moment. Would you be so good as to go along to the scullery and ask the house-maid Simpkins to boil it?

MRS MUMPKIN (*flummoxed*): What – now?

TRENT: If you don't mind. And perhaps you could wait with her to see that she does it straight away. She has a habit of getting – distracted...

MRS MUMPKIN seems to be on the point of objecting strongly – but TRENT holds her gaze firmly for several moments and she finally gets to her feet and goes reluctantly out of the room. TRENT turns his attention back to MR MUMPKIN.

TRENT: Now then, Mr Mumpkin - .

*But MR MUMPKIN motions that TRENT should listen to him.
He wheezes a lot when he speaks but his words are clear
enough.*

MR MUMPKIN: B'ain't no cure for what I got, doctor.

TRENT: I'm sure there is. It's just a question of –

MR MUMPKIN: B'ain't no cure for grey mist.

TRENT: What did you say? I'm sorry? Grey mist?

MR MUMPKIN: Once it gets inside you, that's it. You're finished.

TRENT: But – what exactly is it, this grey mist?

MR MUMPKIN: B'ain't nothing natural, doctor. That's what it is –
and that's for sure.

TRENT: I'm sorry, I'm afraid I don't understand. Where is it?

MR MUMPKIN: It's all around us. And it's nowhere at all. It
b'ain't here all the time like. It's just when –

He breaks off into a wheezing cough.

TRENT: Yes? Just when – ?

MR MUMPKIN: Just when – she comes back.

TRENT (*confused*): Who, Mr Mumpkin? Do you mean – your
wife?

*MR MUMPKIN waves this suggestion away with a wheezing
cough. He seems eager to continue his story.*

MR MUMPKIN: Grey Mist Season, they calls it round here. Can't
say when it'll be coming. Sometimes it don't come for years.
Sometimes it comes in months. But it comes. And when it do
it don't go again until –

He has another fit of coughing.

TRENT: Mr Mumpkin? Until what?

The coughing gradually subsides.

MR MUMPKIN: Until her spite has been fulfilled.

TRENT: I'm sorry. I still don't understand you. Who do you mean?
Who's spite?

MR MUMPKIN: Lived here once, she did. Years ago, that were
mind. Til she took bad, that is. He could've saved her, tis
said, but for what was going on there – between him and her,
like. He were married, you see. He had a wife. And he
wouldn't leave her, no matter how much the girl went on at
him to. Concerned for his reputation, he were, they reckon.
She were at him all the while, the girl. Started to threaten
she'd go to the wife. Tell her what they was up to him, him
and her. (*Coughs*). But then she took bad and he treated her.
And that's when he saw his way out. He could have saved
her, you see. If he'd a mind to. But instead he let her die. It
were the easy way out for him, what with his wife and his
reputation and all – (*coughs again badly*). She were a proud
'un, like, 'tis said. Saw herself in a good place, if she
could've got him. But she were devoted to him too, though.
Thought the world of him. Whereas to him – well, you know
what it's like with these middle-aged toffs – to him she were
just a slip of a girl and a bit of fun for him when his wife
weren't looking.

*He breaks off in another coughing fit while TRENT waits
impatiently. Finally:*

TRENT: I still don't understand. Who, Mr Mumpkin? Who do you
mean?

MR MUMPKIN: The girl's name was –

MRS MUMPKIN (*off*): Here be the hot water you wanted, doctor.

MRS MUMPKIN enters the room explosively with an enamel bowl of hot water. MR MUMPKIN instantly relapses into a wheezing silence, as if determined not to speak again now that his wife has returned.

TRENT: Thankyou, Mrs Mumpkin. Bring it over here. Your husband was telling me about –

MRS MUMPKIN deposits the bowl on the desk then positions herself squarely between TRENT and her husband. It is as if she knows exactly what her husband was telling him about, and is determined to stop it. She gives her husband a fierce look.

MRS MUMPKIN: You don't want to take no notice of he, doctor. Mouth runs away with him, the daft lummox. Talks too much, if you ask me. Never knows when to stop. B'aint that so, Arthur? (*without a pause for confirmation*) Yes. Course it is.

TRENT (*resigned*): Well, let's get on with the examination, shall we?

Blackout

Scene 5

Spotlight illuminates the NARRATOR standing by the armchair DL.
The NARRATOR gives the audience a slight shrug.

NARRATOR: We are reaching the end of the story as I can tell it
to you. As far as Dr Trent was concerned there were a
number of questions he wanted the answers to – a number of
mysteries he couldn't fathom. He had started to feel that the
solutions were all beyond his reach. But he was quite wrong,
I believe. There was really only one mystery. And Dr Trent
was soon to understand its meaning only too well...

Spotlight goes out. The NARRATOR exits the stage.

Lights come up on the main stage. It is evening and once again
the room is only dimly lighted by lamps. The curtains are drawn
over the window. An eerie wind can be heard moaning outside.
It rattles the window frames from time to time. TRENT is seated
at his desk looking through papers. After a moment or two the
rattle of the window frame changes – it becomes the sound of
someone gently tapping the window. TRENT raises his head,
hearing the sound, which immediately stops.

He returns to what he is doing. After another moment the
tapping sound is heard again. TRENT looks around at the
window uncertainly. He gets to his feet. The tapping is heard
again. He goes cautiously towards the window as the tapping
continues, pauses at the curtains – and then pulls one open.
Nobody is there. At the same moment the tapping at the window
is replaced by somebody knocking the consulting room door.

TRENT starts slightly, re-draws the curtain, goes to the door
and opens it. JULIA enters: she has a tray in both hands. It
contains two mugs, a plate with snacks and a bottle of whisky.

JULIA: I thought a nightcap might be a good idea on such a grim
night.

TRENT: That seems like a splendid idea.

She takes the tray to the small table DL and sits in the armchair. TRENT goes to his desk and picks up a buff folder. He glances once at the curtained window. The tapping sound has stopped. Now there is only the low moan of the wind again. He follows JULIA to the table and sits in the upright chair. She uncaps the bottle of whisky and pours a little into each mug, handing him one.

TRENT: Thank you.

JULIA: Something to keep out the chill.

TRENT: It's a miserable night out there.

He taps his mug against hers. They both drink then smile at the warming effect.

JULIA: It's late. You shouldn't still be working.

TRENT: It isn't really work. It's – well you know...

JULIA: You should try to forget all that. You're beginning to look drawn and tired.

TRENT: I wish I could forget it. Somehow I can't. When the Mumpkins were here earlier today –

JULIA: She's a dreadful old harridan! I don't know how he puts up with her.

TRENT: Yes I know. Never stops talking. But today I managed to get her out the room for a few minutes. I told her I needed hot water and asked her to arrange it with Kate and wait while it was done. I told her Kate needed watching...

JULIA: I hope she doesn't find out what you said.

TRENT: So do I. But the rouse worked. The moment his wife was gone Mr Mumpkin began talking. What he told me was – strange – but perhaps it makes some sense. He talked of the grey mist – said that was what was making him ill.

JULIA: But that doesn't make sense – does it?

TRENT: I'm not sure. Not in itself perhaps. It sounded like local superstition again the way he told it – how nobody knows when it's coming or how long it will stay – but that it always comes...

JULIA: It's local folklore, that's all.

TRENT: It's what he told me afterwards though which made me think.

There is a very subtle dimming of the lights in the room for a moment. TRENT and JULIA both shiver.

TRENT: He spoke of some girl from years ago and her love for an older man who was of a higher class. This man was married and clearly in an affair with the girl. The girl wanted him to leave his wife but he refused, afraid for his reputation, partly – but mainly, I suspect, because the girl meant very little to him. Anyway the girl started to threaten him – said she would reveal their affair to his wife if he didn't comply – .

Again the lights dim slightly and they shiver again. There is movement from the corner of the room behind the grandfather clock – VERITY has stepped slowly into the room from the concealed entrance UR of stage. She will remain here in shadow motionless for the next part of the scene, watching them.

JULIA: It's gone cold in here suddenly.

TRENT: A draft from the window, I expect. The frames rattle badly when there's a wind. Anyway, it seems that soon afterwards the girl fell ill and her lover – whoever he was – had the ability to cure her. But he didn't. He saw in her illness a way out of his predicament. And he let her die.

JULIA: That's horrible.

TRENT: Yes, it is. But don't you see, Julia – if he was able to cure her – then he was more than likely a doctor of some kind.

JULIA stares at him, beginning to realise the significance.

JULIA: Who do think this girl was? Did Mr Mumpkin tell you her
     name?

TRENT: He was about to when Mrs Mumpkin arrived with the hot
     water. It was like watching a turtle going back into its shell.
     He just fell silent.

JULIA: But you think the girl might have been – Verity Mandrake?

*At this VERITY moves a step or two further into the room then
stops again, utterly motionless, still watching them. JULIA
shivers again. TRENT seems to have become somehow
uncomfortable. His breathing is slightly ragged.*

TRENT: I thought it was possible, yes. I got rid of the Mumpkins
     as soon as I could – had to find some excuse for the hot
     water, of course. But don't you see, Julia – it would explain
     the missing register -

JULIA: But that would mean – the man she was having the affair
     with – was the doctor here at this practice.

TRENT: I think it has to be, yes. How many others would there be
     in the area who had the ability to cure her and the
     opportunity to kill her without questions being asked?

*JULIA holds her arms. It is not just the thought of this that is
making her cold – it is also the atmosphere of the room. By
contrast TRENT mops his brow. His breathing is still troubled.*

TRENT: After the Mumpkins had left and I had no more patients, I
     decided to go through some of the old cases in the filing
     cabinet – some of the earliest ones. Right at the back of one
     drawer I found this. (*He picks up the buff folder, which is in
     poor condition*) It was crammed inside another folder as if
     someone had attempted to hide it. Look at the name and the
     date on the first sheet.

JULIA takes the folder, opens it and removes the few papers. She looks up at TRENT.

JULIA (*almost whispered*): Verity Mandrake. 1888.

TRENT: Read it.

While JULIA quickly reads the case report, TRENT tries hard to steady his breathing. He pours more whisky into his mug. The bottle rattles against the mug. He takes a deep swallow. VERITY advances another step into the room. JULIA reads several isolated sentences from the report.

JULIA (*reading*): '...such symptoms as I had never encountered before... it must be sufficient to state that the symptoms as diagnosed by myself continually worsened... a varied array of treatments and remedies appeared to have no influence on the patient's affliction... it is therefore with regret that I must conclude that death was inevitable.'

She looks up from the report. TRENT is now in great discomfort. VERITY slowly lifts one arm to point directly at TRENT. It is an accusing gesture.

JULIA: Then it must be true. He allowed her to die and manufactured this report to cover the fact.

TRENT: Look – look at the name - the doctor's –

TRENT can barely get his breath. He stumbles to his feet. JULIA drops the report and stands to assist him. She cannot see Verity.

JULIA: What's wrong? What is it?

TRENT does not answer. Slowly he turns around to face VERITY. He recoils in horror. JULIA tries to console him but he pushes her off.

TRENT: She's there. Look!

JULIA (*seeing nobody*): Who?

TRENT: Don't you see her? Don't you see her? She's there!

JULIA: There's nobody!

TRENT: Just there! Pointing! Accusing! Condemning!

JULIA (*Desparate*): There's no-one! Just us! Come and sit down. You're not well.

She tries to coax TRENT back to the armchair but he pushes her off. She stands terrified. TRENT takes a step closer to VERITY, who remains motionless, her arm still outstretched with the finger pointing directly at him. TRENT can hardly stand or breathe.

TRENT: It's closing in around me. All around me. Like a mist. A grey mist. I can't breathe – can't breathe –

He clutches at his throat as the air seems to be sucked from his lungs. He falls to his knees. VERITY looks down at him. She points down at him. JULIA, in panic, goes to him, takes his shoulders. She stares at VERITY but cannot see her.

JULIA: What is it? What's wrong with you? There's nothing there! Nothing there!

TRENT pushes her away again, then clutches at his chest in a final spasm of suffocation. He collapses to the floor and lies there lifeless. JULIA stares in horror then starts to reel. She faints and falls towards the small table.

From off comes the sound of voices – KATE and CORBY – as they hurry through the house towards the consulting room.

VERITY lowers her arm and backs slowly across the room, back into the concealed stage entrance behind the grandfather clock. She has just gone from view when KATE and CORBY run into

*the room from the door L. They falter just inside the door, then
see the fallen bodies. They advance slowly into the room.*

KATE: Oh my God!

CORBY: Keep your head, woman.

*CORBY bends quickly over TRENT, then moves to examine
JULIA. KATE stands horrified.*

KATE: Are they both – ?

CORBY: Doctor's gone. The girl's breathing. Fainted most like.

KATE: Oh my God. Oh my God!

*CORBY grabs KATE roughly by the arms as she seems on the
point of hysteria. He shakes her.*

CORBY: Keep your head, woman! D'you hear? We've got work to
do!

*KATE calms herself. CORBY is looking around the room. KATE
notices the fallen sheets of paper from the medical report. She
picks up the final sheet and looks at it, then shows it to CORBY.*

KATE: Look at this.

CORBY: What is it?

KATE: Just look. Look at the name and the signature.

*CORBY looks superficially but at that moment JULIA begins to
regain consciousness, moaning slightly. CORBY drops the paper
on the desk and pushes KATE towards JULIA.*

CORBY: Never mind that. We've got to get her out of this room.
Come on. Help me!

*Together they lift JULIA to her feet. Her head hangs forward.
She is still barely conscious. They support her to the door.*

CORBY: You take her from here, woman. Get her into her bed.
    Don't let her back in here. Can you do that?

KATE: Yes.

CORBY: In the morning you'll have to telephone.

KATE: But –

CORBY: I'm no good on those things. You'll do it. Now get her
    away. I'll take care of what's in here. Go on!

*KATE takes JULIA's weight and helps her out of the room.
CORBY closes the door then turns back to the room. He picks
up the rest of the papers from the floor (and anything else that
may have got knocked over in the struggle). He carefully steps
over TRENT'S prone form and goes to put the papers on the
desk. He sees the sheet KATE gave him earlier and picks it up.
He looks at it closely.*

CORBY (*to himself*): The name at the end – Thaddeus Mortimer.

*There is a look of contempt on his face as he drops the sheet
back onto the desk and stoops over TRENT.*

Blackout.

Scene 6

Lights come up on the R stage extension. DR MORTIMER sits at his desk. He has been on the telephone some time. His expression is grave as he listens and occasionally speaks:

MORTIMER: ...Yes... Yes, I see. That is – most unfortunate... Yes, I understand... I will make the necessary arrangements... Thank you for letting me know. You will hear from me in due course... Goodbye.

MORTIMER replaces the receiver slowly. He sits for a moment in deep grim thought. He quells a moment of panic, then gets up from the desk and paces back and forth in agitated consideration. He stares at the portrait on the wall, then calls to an adjoining room:

MORTIMER: Mr Denham! Would you come in here a moment, please!

MORTIMER resumes his seat at the desk, composing himself with effort. DENHAM enters.

DENHAM: Dr Mortimer?

MORTIMER: Some unfortunate news, I'm afraid – concerning Dr Trent. It seems he has – passed away.

DENHAM: Dr Trent? That is very sad news, sir.

MORTIMER: Yes. Very tragic. Heart failure I understand.... The administrator at his practice – a Miss Norbury – is apparently very upset.

DENHAM: Yes, I'm sure. Quite understandable.

MORTIMER: I feel it unwise for her to remain there under the circumstances. I think a stay at a sanatorium might be beneficial to her. Would you kindly arrange it?

DENHAM: Yes, of course, sir.

MORTIMER (*quietly as if to himself*): And we shall need to supply another doctor.

DENHAM: I beg your pardon, sir?

MORTIMER stares briefly into the distance, as if having forgotten DENHAM's presence. Then he returns to reality with affected brisk authority.

MORTIMER: Can you come back in fifteen minutes, please? I shall have a letter for you to post.

DENHAM: Yes, sir.

DENHAM moves towards the door then hesitates.

DENHAM: A most unfortunate business, sir.

MORTIMER appears not to have heard. DENHAM exits. MORTIMER sits quite still as if trying to control panic and fierce emotion. He takes the bottle of pills from his pocket and hastily swallows one. He stands, a little unsteadily, and addresses the portrait on the wall.

MORTIMER: Thaddeus Mortimer – Grandfather... Oh, what did you start all those years ago with your nefarious philandering ways?

MORTIMER sinks back into his chair as if defeated and puts his head in his hands.

Blackout on R extension.

Scene 7

Spotlight comes up on the NARRATOR. He sits on the arm of the chair.

NARRATOR: And that's about it. That is as much of this – ghost story – as I am able to tell. But it isn't the end. No, I'm sure of that. The cycle will go on. The grey mist will continue to fall. The unquiet soul of Verity Mandrake – so cruelly treated by that doctor all those years ago – will endlessly return to the small country medical practice to exact her revenge on the unfortunate incumbent doctor. Until one day – maybe – she feels that her wrath has been sufficiently satiated. And then the grey mist will leave and a sense of peace will fall over that remote piece of England once again. Perhaps. One day. But I shall not see it happen. As I say – this is as much as I can tell you for now. Perhaps – in time – if there's time – I shall be able to tell you more. But for now – (*stands*). But for now you must excuse me. I have an appointment, you see.

Spotlight goes out and the NARRATOR exits the stage. Lights on the main stage come up. It is a bright day some time later. KATE and CORBY are putting finishing touches to tidying the consulting room. There is now no evidence of the horrors that took place there before. KATE looks around the room. CORBY has gone to the window.

KATE: There. That should do it. Everything ready and as it should be.

CORBY: Someone coming.

KATE: What? Is it him? The new doctor?

CORBY: Good chance, I should say.

KATE rushes to the window to peer out, then hurriedly begins to bundle CORBY out of the room.

KATE: Come on, you great lummox! Get yourself away from here! Don't want new doctor put off straight away by the sight of your ugly mug!

CORBY: Stop fussin' me, woman!

KATE: Well off you go then! And keep out of sight!

> *CORBY exits. KATE glances once again around the room. There is a knock at the front door. KATE quickly straightens her dress and apron then exits. The sound of the front door opening is heard and voices off – KATE and the new doctor.*
>
> *KATE brings the new doctor into the consulting room. He is the NARRATOR, carrying a doctor's bag. They move to the centre of the room.*

KATE: Do come in, doctor. Hope you had no trouble finding us?

NARRATOR: No problem at all. It's a very pleasant walk from the railway station.

KATE: This is the consulting room.

NARRATOR: So I see.

KATE: Medicine chest in the corner. Shelves of reference books. Your – doctor's chair and desk.

> *The NARRATOR takes a moment to look at his surroundings. Then he smiles in satisfaction.*

NARRATOR: Very good. A nice airy room. Yes. You know – I think I'm going to like it here.

> *The NARRATOR suddenly stops and shivers.*

VERITY (*voice off*): Help me.

> *Blackout.*
>
> *CURTAIN*

—THE GREY MIST STAGE PLAN—

NB: in the original production the side set was finally positioned on the opposite side to put greater distance between the two 'offices'.

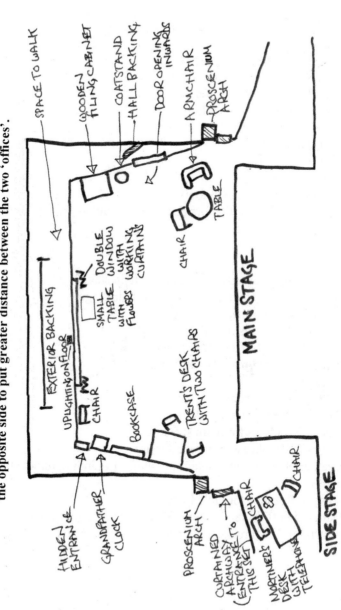

Furniture and Properties List

Main Stage:
Doctor's desk
Doctor's chair
Upright chairs x2
Floor-standing bookcase
Grandfather clock (full height)
Curtains at window (working)
Wooden filing cabinet
Coat stand
Occasional table
Armchairs x2
Small low table (by window)
Working lamps x3 (doctors desk / filing cabinet / small table)
Mirror on wall

Side Stage:
Doctor's desk (smarter than one on main stage)
Doctor's chair (smarter than one on main stage)
Visitor's chair (upright)
Telephone (old fashioned)
Portrait on wall of Thaddeus Mortimer
Papers and one or two books for desk

Sundry Stage Props
Papers for main stage desk
Doctor's gadgets for main stage desk
Books for bookcase (reference style)
Leather photo album containing photos (including removable Verity photo)
Vase of flowers (for table by window)
Battered buff folder containing papers (for filing cabinet)
Several medical registers (stiff-backed exercise books)

Personal and Specific Props Act 1

Sc 1: Smoking jacket (Narrator)
   Duster (Kate)
   Doctor's bag (Trent)
   Overcoat (Trent)
   Scarf (Trent)
   Tray with teacups x2 / teapot / milk jug / sugar bowl / spoons x2

Sc 3: Stethoscope (Trent)
   Teacup and saucer (smashable!)
   Mop and bucket (Kate)

Sc 4: Glass of port
   Plate with cheese and biscuits

Sc 5: Prescription form 1920s style (Trent)

Sc 6: Outdoor coat (Julia)
   Muffins on plate
   Side plates x2
   Plate with butter
   Butter knife
   Tray with tea things - as in Scene 1
   Handkerchief (Trent)

Sc 7: Draughts board and pieces
   Beer glasses x2
   Large jug containing beer
   'Local Folklore' book (on bookshelves)

Personal and Specific Props Act 2

Sc 1: Extra papers (Trent's desk)
   Paper with 'Verity Mandrake' handwritten on it many times
   Duster (Kate)
   Child's sketch
   Photo of Verity (removed from leather photo album)

Sc 2: Fake blood (Corby)
   Enamel bowl containing water (Kate)
   Roll of bandage (Julia)

      Scissors (Julia)
      Bottle of antiseptic (Julia)

Sc 3: Sling (Corby)
      Tea things / muffins etc - as in Act 1 sc 6

Sc 4: Enamel bowl of water – as in Sc 2 (Mrs Mumpkin)

Sc 5: Mugs x2
      Plate of 'snacks'
      Bottle of whisky
      Battered buff folder containing papers (see Sundry Props)

Sc 7: Doctor's bag and overcoat (Narrator)

LIGHTING PLOT

ACT 1

Scene 1: At start main stage and side stage in darkness. Spotlight on Narrator

Cue 1: Narrator: 'Yes it's beginning now' (p.6) – Spotlight out. Lights fade up on main stage to represent afternoon

Cue 2: Trent exits, Kate enters (p.14) – Lighting fades very gradually to indicate dusk closing in during sequence with Kate

Cue 3: Julia: 'Quite a looker' (p.16) – Slow blackout on main stage

Scene 2

Cue 4: Lights up on side stage (p.17)

Cue 5: Mortimer puts his head in his hands (p.20) –

Quick blackout on side stage

Scene 3

Cue 6: Spotlight on Narrator (p.21)

Cue 7: Narrator 'For now' (p.21) – Spotlight out. Lights up on main stage to represent morning

Cue 8: Trent 'I'm coming' (p.31) – Quick blackout

Scene 4

Cue 9: Lights partially up on main stage to represent evening / prop lamps are lit here and there on stage (p.32)

Cue 10: Kate 'It's happening again' (p.35) – Quick blackout

Scene 5

Cue 11: Spotlight on Narrator (p.36)

Cue 12: Narrator '...reassuring routine' (p.36) – Spotlight out. Lights up on main stage to represent a bright morning

Cue 13: Trent 'I don't know!' (p.48) – Quick blackout

Scene 6

Cue 14: Lights up on main stage to represent late afternoon / dusk through window (p.49)

Cue 15: Trent laughs then composes himself (p.53) – Quick blackout

Scene 7

Cue 16: Lights partially up on main stage to represent night / prop lamps are lit throwing most of the stage into semi-darkness (p.54)

Cue 17: Trent pulls back curtain revealing Verity (p.61) – Verity is starkly lit from below

Cue 18: Trent puts his hands to his face (p.61) – Instant blackout

ACT 2

Scene 1: At start, main stage and side stage in darkness, spotlight on Narrator

Cue 1: Narrator '...he examined it closely' (p.62) – Spotlight out / Lights fade up on main stage to represent afternoon

Cue 2: Trent 'Who was Verity Mandrake. I have to know' (p.71) – Quick blackout

Scene 2

Cue 3: Spotlight on Narrator (p.72)

Cue 4: Narrator 'Personally I don't think it would' (p.72) – Spotlight out / Lights up dimly on main stage / prop lamps lit / dark outside window

Cue 5: Julia switches on main room light (p.75) – Brighten stage lighting

Cue 6: Trent switches off lamp on desk (p.80) – Simultaneous instant blackout on main stage

Scene 3

Cue 7: Lights up on main stage to represent late afternoon (p.81)

Cue 8: Trent 'The same year as the missing medical register' (p.86)
 - Quick blackout main stage

Scene 4

Cue 9: Lights up on main stage to represent morning (p.87)

Cue 10: Trent 'Let's get on with the examination shall we?' (p.90)
 – Slow blackout

Scene 5

Cue 11: Spotlight on Narrator (p.91)

Cue 12: Narrator '...understand its meaning only too well' (p.91) –
 Spotlight out / lights up on main stage – dim lighting / prop
 lamps on

Cue 13: Trent 'It's what he told me afterwards...' (p.93) - Slight
 dimming of main stage lights

Cue 14: Trent 'If he didn't comply' (p.93) - Main stage lights dim a
 little more

Cue 15: Corby begins to stoop over Trent (p.98) – Quick blackout

Scene 6

Cue 16: Lights up on side stage (p.99)

Cue 17: Mortimer 'What did you start with your nefarious ways?'
 (p.100) – Slow fade to black

Scene 7

Cue 18: Spotlight on Narrator (p.101)

Cue 19: Narrator 'I have an appointment you see' (p.101) –
 Spotlight out / lights up on main stage to represent bright
 daylight

Cue 20: Verity 'Help Me' (p.102) – Slow blackout

SOUND EFFECTS PLOT

ACT 1

Cue 1: Julia 'We can expect Dr Trent...' (p.9) – Door knocker

Cue 2: Kate exits (p.9) – Front door opens

Cue 3: Julia 'Take care on your way back to the station' (p.14) – Front door closes / footsteps returning

Cue 4: from start of Scene 4 (p.32) – Low wind moaning. Verity whimpering

Cue 5: Trent studies a particular photo in the album (p.32) – Verity's voice 'Help me'

Cue 6: Trent exits, Kate listens (p.34) – Footsteps climbing stairs

Cue 7: Trent is about to take the photo album from the shelf (p.41) – Drone effect – continues until Trent leaves the room.

Cue 8: Julia 'They're coming back in' (p.42) – Footsteps entering hall / front door closes

Cue 9: Corby 'He had his own carriage...' (p.58) – Low wind moaning – to end of scene, gradually building in volume

Cue 10: Trent falls into deep sleep – pause – then (p.60) – Verity whimpering. Verity's voice (see script for exact positioning of SFX)

Cue 11: Trent 'Verity Mandrake' and stares towards window (p.61) – Drone effect

Cue 12: Trent pulls back curtain revealing Verity (p.61) – Female scream

ACT 2

Cue 1: Julia '...written again and again. Dr Trent?' (p.63) – Footsteps in hall

Cue 2: Julia 'Mandrake – Mandrake', about to open drawer (p.63) – Footsteps on gravel path

Cue 3: Trent at desk sits straight, gasps, shivers (p.73) – Verity's voice 'Help me. Please. Help me'

Cue 4: Trent 'There's a gap in the dates' (p.73) – Drone effect – until Verity withdraws from sight on p.74

Cue 5: Trent approaches window (p.74) – Male cry of agony (or this could be done live)

Cue 6: Trent exits stage (p.74) – Front door opens / front door closes

Cue 7: Corby 'That's just the way it is' (p.81) – Front door opens

Cue 8: As main stage lights come up (p.91) – Wind moaning / rattling window frames. Tapping on window - as rattling window frames sfx stops (see stage directions in script)

Cue 9: Trent '...if he didn't comply' (p.93) – Drone effect – as Verity enters until she exits on p.96

Cue 10: Corby exits, Kate looks around room (p.102) – Door knocker

Cue 11: Kate exits (p.102) – Front door opens / front door closes

Cue 12: After Narrator shivers (p.102) – Verity 'Help Me'

Lightning Source UK Ltd.
Milton Keynes UK
UKHW010233221118
332740UK00005B/573/P